ESPRESSO!

ESPRESSO!

Starting and Running
Your Own Specialty Coffee Business

Joe Monaghan and Julie Sheldon Huffaker

John Wiley & Sons, Inc.
New York • Chichester • Brisbane • Toronto • Singapore

Publisher: *Peggy Burns*
Editor: *Claire Thompson*
Managing Editor: *Allison Morvay*
Editorial Production: *Julie S. Huffaker*

This text is printed on acid-free paper.

This publication is designed to provide accurate and authoritative
information in regard to the subject matter covered. It is sold with the
understanding that the publisher is not engaged in rendering legal,
accounting, or other professional services. If legal advice or expert
assistance is required, the services of a competent professional person
should be sought.

Library of Congress Cataloging-in-Publication Data:
Monaghan, Joe.
    Espresso!:starting and running your own specialty coffee business/
by Joe Monaghan and Julie Sheldon Huffaker.
        p.   cm.
    Includes index.
    ISBN 0-471-12138-X (paper : alk. paper)
    1. Coffeehouses--Management. 2. Espresso. 3. New business
enterprises--Management.   I. Huffaker, Julie Sheldon, 1967–
II. Title.
TX911.3.M27M66 1995
647.95'068--dc20

                                                        95-17895

Printed in the United States of America
10 9 8 7 6 5

To Kent Bakke, who taught me the true meaning of
dedication and perseverance, and without whom
I would not be in this business.

And to Denise, Kendall, and Sean,
who make life itself possible.

—J.M.

With great appreciation for all of the elementary school teachers,
loan officers, exotic dancers, biologists, and
municipal workers who stepped into
my world as I made their lattes.

—J.S.H.

CONTENTS

PREFACE

What makes a successful business? Time, energy, and a good idea.

For more and more enterprising individuals, selling espresso offers the perfect proposition. Espresso can be profitable, flexible, and fun as a stand-alone business, as well as providing additional value to an existing retail or restaurant operation.

First of all, you may ask: what exactly is espresso? Espresso is an Italian coffee-brewing method that's been around for about a hundred years. Perfected to a science in its motherland, espresso was initially introduced to the United States in the mid-1950s. It first appeared, not surprisingly, in the cloistered Italian neighborhoods of large urban areas.

The next American audience to appreciate espresso was the clientele of the smoke-filled beatnik coffeehouse. By all accounts, their strain of espresso was not very tasty. Both technology and expertise have improved greatly since that time.

In the late 1970s, things started to change in a hurry. Upscale restaurants, though they began with little espresso-brewing aptitude, began to list espresso beverages on their menus. Pacific Northwest retail giant Nordstrom jumped onto the scene in the early 1980s with a national string of coffee carts. Starbucks Coffee Company and SBC (Seattle's Best Coffee), both headquartered in Seattle, developed the "coffee bar" concept there. The immediate service offered by these coffee bars was instantly appealing. Patrons could walk in, buy a quality cup of coffee, and leave.

Espresso became a popular after-dinner treat, a sound social alternative to the more traditional bar scene. It was easy to convince the public to go out for espresso; good espresso is difficult to replicate at home. Slight differences in preparation make for great differences in taste. Most devotees can pinpoint their favorite bar—even their favorite barista, or espresso "bartender"—without thinking twice.

The average selling price of a latte in the 1980s was $1.00. Today, the same drink sells for $1.50 or more. For a luxury item, however, espresso beverages have always been relatively affordable—as is evidenced by the diverse mix of people who stand in line every morning to purchase them. Coffee drinkers consider their cappuccino a treat, and can manage to buy it daily. It gives them a lift, because there is the caffeine factor, of course, along with a dose of upbeat human contact and a quick, excusable moment "off."

Coffee is one of the hottest commodities on the world market, second only to oil in volume of trade. In fact, the United States imports more coffee beans than any other country. The bulk of this coffee is referred to as "institutional" coffee. While consumption of this type of coffee, and coffee consumption as a whole, has been decreasing since the 1950s, the enjoyment and sales of gourmet coffees have increased steadily.

Institutional-type coffee typically features mediocre to poor beans—usually *robusta* beans, the low-grown, highly disease resistant, and less expensive of the two commercially viable coffee species. Institutional coffee is roasted and brewed in large quantities. Caffeine, rather than taste, is its primary selling point. This type of coffee is not often considered a profit center. Instead, the coffee is marketed as a "bottomless cup," or sold for $.05 or $.10 a fill.

The gourmet segment of the market is known as "specialty" coffee. In general, specialty coffee is earmarked by its superior raw materials (primarily *arabica* beans), scrupulous blending and roasting, and careful preparation. The growing popularity of espresso fuels the gourmet coffee boom; espresso beverages are our primary focus throughout this book. The espresso method of extraction itself is a highly specialized process, bringing the rich tastes of coffee under a microscope. Espresso brewing subjects finely ground coffee to high temperature and extreme pressure, coaxing the fullest flavor, the "heart" of the coffee, into the brew—a truly spiritual experience for the coffee lover!

Think of espresso not as any one drink, but as a category of coffee beverages. The foundation for these beverages is the coffee itself, intense and thick, brewed in one-ounce servings on an espresso machine. An espresso beverage is a custom drink, made with espresso coffee for an individual customer. Hot, cold, milky, straight—the capacity for specialization is what makes espresso such a great experience. As an espresso customer, you define your own drink.

Selling espresso is a good way to have fun while generating income, and as a business venture it can go far beyond simply earning a living. You can get started in the business with a relatively small investment and realize a sizable profit per drink. The high profit margin and overall affordability of the specialty coffee business make it almost recession-proof. Not only does the selling price of the beverage absorb sudden increases in the cost of its components—milk, for example—but history shows that the coffee business thrives even during hard economic times.

The specialty coffee business is a good one but, like all good business prospects, requires careful consideration. This book will first lead you through the steps of evaluating whether or not espresso is a viable venture for you—and if so, which form of the business best suits your goals. Then, we'll tell you exactly how to make your choice a success.

Welcome to the world of espresso.

JOE MONAGHAN

JULIE SHELDON HUFFAKER

ACKNOWLEDGMENTS

There is no one roaster, machine distributor, retail operator, or coffee lover who can be awarded absolute credit for giving birth to the specialty coffee industry. Specialty coffee is a social and collaborative business, the dynamic product of everyone involved.

That said, there are several dedicated individuals whose passion and integrity have been instrumental in shaping the North American espresso experience. Their vision, foresight, and tremendous energy make great espresso possible for aficionados and entrepreneurs around the country.

Since constructing the Emerald City's very first espresso cart, Kent Bakke and John Blackwell have dedicated their professional lives to the rich Italian tradition of espresso. Their standards are uncompromising, their pursuit of quality infinite.

Brenna Worthen, Kate Higgens, Vinnie Horiuchi, John Hogard, and Matt Montgomery of Espresso Specialists, Inc., have each contributed immeasurably to forming a uniquely expert and compassionate espresso business entity. We pay tribute, as well, to David Schomer of Espresso Vivace and Kevin Knox of Allegro Coffee Company—two fervid individuals who are not simply maintaining industry standards, but actively setting them.

We acknowledge all who bring their own passion and desire for quality to the espresso industry. These people understand: when you care about what you do, and you do it well, success inadvertently follows.

We extend heartfelt thanks to those stalwart souls who have supported the evolution of this book to its present form. Thanks to Leslie Bevan for her unwaveringly positive attitude, her editorial contributions, and for all those dinners delivered computerside. Laura Sommers and Dennis Monaghan, we thank you for your enduring support and graphics assistance. We are grateful for the keen eyes and constructive comments of Brandy K. Poirier, and thank both Brandy and Lisa McCrummen for their valuable contributions to the public relations section.

Finally, we wish to take advantage of this opportunity to thank our editor at John Wiley & Sons, Claire Thompson, for believing in our book and shepherding the manuscript so expertly—and gracefully—to completion.

Partners, colleagues, and friends, we couldn't have done it without you.

CHAPTER 1
Choosing the Right Espresso Opportunity

There is a wide range of business opportunities that involve espresso. This chapter will review some of the pros and cons of each. We encourage you to select the espresso venture that best suits your personal and financial goals.

In general, espresso opportunities fall into one of three main categories. The first is the business which has espresso as its main focus. The second can be described as a business to which espresso is added to complement existing services. Finally, there is the business which focuses on specialty coffee and incorporates espresso as part of its overall coffee program.

The Business with Espresso as Its Primary Focus

This category includes espresso carts, espresso concessions or catering, espresso drive through operations, and the more permanent espresso bars or coffee houses. In Seattle, often heralded as "Latteland," the vast majority of espresso outlets take the form of the latter.

CART/KIOSK

Simply said, an espresso cart is a box on wheels that supports espresso-brewing equipment. Typically, carts make a variety of espresso and noncoffee beverages (hot cocoa, steamed milk,

1

Italian sodas) while offering pastries, confections, and other coffee complements.

A kiosk is a similar structure that has expanded physically in size and function. Like carts, kiosks are free-standing. They can be mobile, but generally feature solid counters—and more of them—as well as extensive overhead signage and additional cases or shelving for display. The investment for these operations is higher; they tend to be situated in high-volume areas like the centers of malls and airport terminals. For the purposes of this section, both carts and kiosks will be referred to simply as carts.

Where location is concerned, espresso carts are extremely flexible. A cart can dovetail into the tiniest niche and still be a marvelous success, opening to thrive as a business one day where there wasn't anything the day before. Espresso carts are easy to operate and manage, and have very straightforward inventory requirements. In most cases, the owner is the operator.

Financially, an espresso cart requires a minimal up-front investment: around $15,000. A cart can be a strong entree to larger opportunities, allowing the owner to build the working capital and reputation of his business until the perfect opportunity for retail or site expansion presents itself. An entrepreneur who operates a cart can take advantage of the specialty coffee trend without dramatic financial risk. And the potential for profit is considerable.

There is tremendous earning potential in expansion to multiple sites. While the single site owner/operator characteristically enjoys—and has a talent for—the face-to-face requirements of running a cart, such as customer interaction, expansion requires a fair measure of personnel and business management expertise.

Typically, single cart operators underestimate the scope of work required to grow a business. Many find themselves struggling with hats they were trying to avoid wearing in the first place. Along those same lines, the person who excels in the big business side of things isn't usually the best person behind the bar. If you want to expand your business, make all decisions with that in mind.

The same mobility that works in favor of the cart also works against it. The single biggest drawback to cart operations is that landlords have a hard time seeing them as permanent. The first espresso cart in Seattle, Monorail Espresso, now sits in its fifth or sixth location. Fortunately for the operator, his clientele keeps moving right along with it!

Other negatives include inclement weather for those carts situated outdoors, a limited ability to present products (read: no space), and the long period of time it may take to build the business to a truly profitable level. You have to sell a lot of drinks to pay the rent, and you'll build your clientele one drink at a time.

Some cities flat out don't allow cart businesses, in part because the reputation of other cart type operations pegs them as undependable. Even where carts are allowed, there are a number of building and health codes that can be difficult to overcome. Many of these reach beyond the business itself—such as the necessity of having a viable commissary, for example, or the guidelines about where a cart can be stored.

The final hurdle is competition. Carts are extremely vulnerable to it: they can be outnumbered by the advent of a major chain of retail stores, swamped by other carts, or booted out by the landlord who decides your business is so successful that he'll just set up his own.

SPECIAL EVENTS/CATERING/CONCESSIONS

A special event espresso service is a mobile operation, and serves coffee at—you guessed it—special events. These may include music concerts, food fairs, basketball games, or corporate parties. An espresso concessions operation usually involves a semi-permanent cart, kiosk, van, or trailer at a special events center, such as a sporting arena or movie theater.

These designations can refer to a huge range of possible outfits, from a cart hauled from event to event to a sophisticated conglomeration of supplies and services inside a large tent. The larger operations are capable of serving upwards of 5,000–6,000 cups a day.

An espresso catering operation is also event-oriented, but is usually contracted as part of an overall catering service for weddings, parties, business conventions, and the like. The espresso operator is typically hired by a food caterer to work a specific event. This means there are fewer health department regulations to meet independently, but usually not enough business to act as a sole source of income.

DRIVE-THROUGH

We live in a car-driven society, so why not? Many drive-through espresso stands were once photo developing booths or fast food joints. Others are mobile trailers plunked down in the corner of grocery store parking lots.

The operation of a drive-through is similar to that of a cart or kiosk. The product mix is pretty much the same, but a drive-through markets almost exclusively to commuters in cars. The arrangement of a drive-through, incidentally, should facilitate passing drinks into the driver's side window. The best possible scenario is a booth offering easy auto access on both sides.)

The primary advantage to this type of operation is its overall simplicity. Good location, and customer access to it, are crucial— and hard to find. Start-up investment ranges from $15,000 to $250,000, the higher amount including funds for fixed plumbing, speaker phones, and other snazzy fixtures.

Perhaps most discouraging is a dilemma posed by the health department: should a drive-through be classified as a mobile operation, or as a permanent fixture? The latter introduces a new host of guidelines that must be followed to the letter. Make a thorough exploration of health department issues before committing to a drive-through venture.

ESPRESSO BAR/COFFEEHOUSE

In this book, we use the terms "espresso bar" and "coffeehouse" interchangeably. Please note that the coffeehouse of which we speak is one that focuses its beverage efforts on espresso. (Coffeehouses in some parts of the country serve drip-brewed coffee as their primary beverage.) Espresso bars are different from specialty coffee stores in that espresso is their primary product. Because they have the luxury of space, espresso bars may serve a variety of food items as well, from breakfast pastries to full-service lunches, soups, or baked goods.

An espresso bar has a fixed location with a long-term lease, and thus greater potential to build a market. It is essentially a large kiosk or enclosed retail space, ranging in size from 800 to 1,500 square feet (sometimes more) and with a fair amount of seating.

An espresso bar offers greater opportunity for creative use of space and design than does a cart. Espresso bars and coffeehouses tend to be destination spots, rather than impulse or convenience stops. They draw groups of customers for social reasons, and they also attract business-type gatherings.

As you might expect, the financial commitment for starting an espresso bar is large—usually somewhere between $50,000 and $150,000—and staffing requirements are high. Hours of operation are long; most coffeehouses open their doors in early morning and stay active until late at night. This poses a problem: how do you fill the "dead" times in between? This quandary is often tackled through the addition of an attractive food menu. Good idea, but remember: where operations are concerned, an espresso bar faces many of the same expenses as a restaurant, but ticket items are substantially lower.

Location is a large part of the overall financial commitment; any "leasehold" improvement to the property made by the lessor is owned by the landlord. Unlike an espresso cart, you can't take this investment with you.

Espresso as an Add-On Service

This is the largest overall category of espresso business. These "add-on" ventures take many forms, which can be broken down yet further into food and nonfood ventures. The greatest potential downfall of an add-on operation is lack of attention paid to beverage quality. Do not underestimate the need for significant training of *all* employees who may prepare drinks for customers.

Espresso Added to Food Service

Despite the rapid growth of espresso-focused operations, there are still more espresso programs found linked to larger food services than anywhere else. From the restaurant that puts espresso on its dinner menu to the small yogurt or fresh-baked cookie shop, espresso can bring significant revenue and foot traffic to an existing food service.

Restaurants often have drip coffee machines because they think they have to. In the past, coffee has been considered a loss-leader, a necessary evil of sorts. The profitability of espresso gives the restauranteur an opportunity to increase the ticket price while enhancing her establishment's image, making a positive impression on customers at the end of the dinner. Espresso is also a good alternative to alcohol. An espresso menu provides a valuable mechanism for marketing, and allows a restaurant owner to capitalize on a growing trend. ·

The logistics of serving fine espresso in a restaurant bear careful consideration. In an environment where quick turnover and a large staff are the norm, the restaurant manager must decide how to ensure consistent and high-quality preparation. Routine maintenance of the espresso machine is also an issue.

A pre-existing emphasis on quality food is a significant advantage. Will the entire staff be trained to use the machine, and be expected to make espresso drinks for their own individual customers? Or will the espresso machine sit in the bar area, the sole domain of the bartender—a role bartenders historically resist? You can also hire and train a special barista who makes drinks as needed. This is optimal, but not particularly practical.

Finally, there's the question of machine size. Should you buy a larger and more expensive machine, one capable of serving everyone in a party of eight at the same time? The machine that can do this is probably much more machine than your restaurant will need to meet demand throughout the rest of the day.

Nonrestaurant food services such as yogurt or cookie stores are free to concentrate on the specialty nature of espresso. They have the time and space to offer a more involved menu and one-on-one service. Many of these businesses were originally founded on specialty trends; as a result, their existing clientele is ripe for the concept, willing to spend the extra money for specialty items. Several of these trends have run their course—sales aren't necessarily dropping off, but they are leveling—so espresso can prove to be a cost-effective business enhancement. However: these businesses, too, face training, investment, and operational issues. Is there enough space for the yogurt machine, the espresso machine, and an extra refrigerator? Can you staff enough people to make lattes during the lunch rush?

ESPRESSO ADDED TO A NONFOOD BUSINESS

Nonfood business ventures where espresso can prove successful include bookstores, clothing stores, gas stations, dry cleaners... the possibilities are endless. Because some site facilities already exist, overhead will probably be lower than the amount one incurs with a cart or kiosk. Espresso can function as a marketing draw to the primary focus through free drink offers, coupons, or simple availability and convenience. Essentially, any operation with a clientele of ready coffee drinkers and a commitment to beverage quality can make espresso a profitable addition.

But be realistic about the challenges. Nonfood operations may have more difficulty lining up the proper health permits and facilities. Or, the existing business may house delicate items around which coffee cups might be unwelcome.

Carefully evaluate the compatibility of your market: will the patrons of a pet store really go for the idea? How about the scheduled customers of an auto body shop? You may have a limited window of business.

Remember that espresso is a highly specialized, handmade drink, requiring time for interaction with the customer as well as preparation. Does your business allow for this kind of prolonged contact? Consider the skills and interests of your current staff. Even if your customers are open to the idea, there may be resistance within the business—particularly if your employees aren't already "food people."

Espresso and the Specialty Coffee Outlet/Cafe

The specialty coffee outlet is generally a store of 600 to 1,500 square feet which sells a variety of fresh-roasted, specialty ("gourmet") coffee beans. The business either has a roaster or has purchased roasted coffees from a separate roaster for resale. The product mix may include teas, fresh foodstuffs like locally baked pastries and breads, and other gourmet food items and accessories. Typically, coffee hardware and home-brewing devices are also for sale to encourage and educate customers about their home consumption of coffee.

Starting from scratch, the cost to establish a specialty coffee outlet is high: about $75,000 to $300,000. The degree of expertise and experience required is also very high, particularly if coffee roasting is going to be part of the operation. If you don't already, plan to take your coffee very seriously.

Adding espresso to an existing specialty coffee operation costs even less than establishing a cart. Buy a machine and grinder—plus any additional plumbing and cabinet fittings, inventory, and design expenditures—and you're in business. The fact that your staff is already sensitized to the educational and sales issues surrounding specialty coffee products is of great advantage.

The retailer should not forget, however, that introducing espresso is like adding an entirely new branch of operations. Personnel management, inventory control, and sales training are only part of what it takes to succeed with espresso.

The function of the espresso bar is threefold. First, it acts as a legitimate profit center; while the espresso bar in such a place may generate a comparatively small portion of the total revenue, espresso drinks do offer the highest profit center per square foot. The retail business already draws a coffee-loving customer base, and they are of course a great potential source of espresso sales.

Second, espresso provides an engaging means for educating customers. It also spurs the sale of other consumables and retail hardware. The retail store becomes a destination and, wooed by espresso beverages, new customers will soon concentrate all their coffee purchasing there.

A specialty coffee outlet is a fairly permanent proposition, offering stable facilities and a long-term lease. Conventional landlords and property managers tend to be more comfortable with this idea than with other espresso concepts.

Management and training for a larger staff can be a challenge. Inventory requirements also increase with space, as does the list of necessary product suppliers. The outlet owner is sitting on an investment of significantly higher dollar value, which can impinge on her flexibility to take advantage of future expansion prospects.

To Franchise or Not to Franchise?

A franchise is the right granted by a company to an individual or group to market and sell the company's products in a specific locale. There are pros and cons associated with going into business as part of a franchise operation. In general, franchisers will propose the advantages of a pre-established identity, pre-determined operational procedures, and large-scale marketing. Some espresso cart franchise operations provide ongoing assistance, including the security of a "sure bet" location.

What do the franchise companies want in return? Income. Ask yourself whether or not you're willing to part with it. Many people are attracted to the espresso business because they want the independence of running their own show. They're willing to invest time and energy in order to claim the profits. Weigh the cost against the benefit: what a franchiser is going to charge versus what he's giving you.

The growing number of franchise opportunities in the espresso industry include cart operations, kiosks, espresso bars, and full-blown coffee bean stores. They are starting to establish useful name recognition. But while franchisers may offer a bundle of start-up and operations information, there is plenty available elsewhere—of equal or greater benefit and for a significantly lower expenditure. You're holding a sterling example right here in your hands.

Chapter 2, which takes you through the stages of assembling a business plan, will further acquaint you with your own business vision. This provides you with a constitution of sorts against which to measure the franchising decision, and others like it.

Put careful thought into your own needs before jumping into a business proposition. Talk to people who have already undertaken what you're in the process of considering. Beware the fast-talking salesperson who isn't necessarily looking out for your long-term best interests.

Consider lifestyle, budget, expertise, possible location, and the physical requirements that go along with each espresso concept. Above all, go with your gut. Use the planning process we've outlined to evaluate your business options, and remember: proper planning is crucial to success, no matter what scope of operation you intend to launch.

The ultimate key to success in all cases is quality. Anyone can buy a machine and pull shots of brown water. Even the best coffee and the finest equipment will only get you halfway there. Pay serious attention to beverage quality so that your investment will pay for itself—and more.

Checklist: Choosing the Right Opportunity

____ **Understand the different types of espresso operations**

    ____ Espresso-focused business

        ____ Cart/kiosk

        ____ Special events/catering/concessions

        ____ Drive-through

        ____ Espresso bar

    ____ Espresso added to existing business concept

        ____ Addition to food service

        ____ Addition to non-food business

    ____ Specialty coffee outlet/café

____ **Begin defining your own vision**

    ____ What is your vision for the business? For future expansion?

    ____ Is this your main source of income or a sideline?

    ____ If you are adding espresso to an existing business, how do you see the two working together?

    ____ What, if any, espresso businesses already exist in your area? How mature is the market?

    ____ Which concepts are/will be most successful in your area? Why?

    ____ Where will your customers come from? What will bring them to you?

    ____ Approximately how much capital will you have to invest?

____ **Choose the concept that best fits your goals and market**

(If you're not ready to do this yet, don't worry. The next several chapters will take you through the steps of refining your business vision, securing a sound location, and finding the financing you'll need. Understanding those steps will help you to determine which espresso concept best suits your individual situation and market.)

CHAPTER 2
Getting Down to Business

To get a good start in the espresso business, there are a few things a potential business owner simply must have.

First and foremost, an entrepreneur in the espresso business must have determination. There will be obstacles to overcome. In addition, an espresso entrepreneur must have the confidence that his or her business is worthwhile. Abundant energy and a sound commitment to pursuing the process carefully, eliminating as many pitfalls as possible, are also elements essential to a successful business start-up. Proper planning is critical, regardless of your business direction.

Developing a Business Plan

If you're thinking of beginning a totally new business, prepare a thorough and complete business plan. A business plan has many purposes, and should be taken seriously. They can be instrumental in securing loans or other funding, attracting business partners, and doing ground-level troubleshooting.

Even if you're planning to add espresso to an existing business, you need to do this planning. Logistically, how will espresso fit into your business? What new vendors do you need? Once this exciting beverage is available on your premises, how will you promote it?

All businesses begin with a plan of some sort, whether this plan finds its genesis on paper, in one's head, or on coffeehouse napkins. If you take the time to document an organized business plan, however, your business will come a lot closer to what you want it to be. Businesses have a tendency to take on lives of their own. And, although structuring a business plan may seem less exciting than approaching a landlord or buying an espresso machine, do it first. This primary step is critical to your success.

A comprehensive business plan for any type of specialty coffee venture should include the following:

Executive Summary
- General statement of purpose and objectives of the business
- Definition of the market served
- Description of the products and/or services offered
- Financial summary

Market Evaluation
- Customer profiles (for example, workers, commuters, students, hospital staff and visitors, etc.)
- Projected frequency of purchase
- Price and customer sensitivity to change
- Income/education of customer base
- Competition

Products and Services
- Detailed description
- Sample menu, formatted nicely for presentation purposes

Management Team
- Description of qualifications
- Functions

Operations
- Location
- Facilities required
- Equipment required
- Staffing requirements (with an organizational chart that illustrates the division of responsibilities)
- Training requirements (initial and ongoing)

Marketing Strategy (strategies to build customer base)
- Location
- Advertising and promotional programs
- Product quality

Financial Analysis
- Projected start-up costs
- Operating capital requirements
- Method of providing capital
- 3–5 year profit/loss projections

Risk Analysis
- Primary areas of risk
- Viable steps for dealing with them, should the business encounter difficulties

What exactly do you want your business to be? How will it affect your life? The lives of the people close to you? Are you willing to work outside traditional business hours? What social value does your business need to have? Are you planning expansion?

If the vision is not carefully planned, your task list will snowball. The prospect of beginning this business—which once held such appeal—may quickly become overwhelming and unmanageable. A business plan will help you organize your course of action, arranging the pieces into a logical sequence of events.

Helpful outlines for a thorough business plan can be obtained through the local chapter of the SBA (Small Business Administration), with additional and free guidance available from a SCORE (Society of the Corps of Retired Business Executives) representative. Other aids and references can be found under "Starting a Business" in your local library.

Defining your Business Identity

Coming up with a name and logo for your business will help you engage in a little positive visualization (and a little goes a long way). The presentation of a name and polished logo will also help to establish a certain trustworthiness for your business right up front. If you've never worked with one, the yellow pages are full of graphic designers who can turn your business name into a tight, impressive imprint for letterhead and proposals.

A strong business identity buys significant credibility, particularly with landlord and investor types. This might not be a bad time to have business cards made up, too; you'll find plenty of uses for them, and the cards will increase your credibility still further. An official business name, logo, and materials will make proposals look more professional, your ideas more promising.

If you're adding espresso to your business, the main argument for an espresso-specific logo or name is the extent to which you can capitalize on the identity your establishment already enjoys. Start thinking about this aspect of the venture early, and nourish your image. The identity of your espresso bar should be strong enough to act like an attractive personality within your business, complementing existing services and drawing customers like a magnet.

Logo courtesy of Mocha Joe's Espresso

Checklist: Getting Down to Business

____ **Develop your business plan, including:**

    ____ Executive summary

    ____ Market evaluation

    ____ Description of products and services

    ____ Management team

    ____ Operations

    ____ Marketing strategy

    ____ Financial analysis

    ____ Risk analysis

____ **Define your business identity**

    ____ Establish business name and logo

    ____ Design and produce business cards and other materials

CHAPTER 3
Location,
Location, Location

The most critical choice you have to make when starting a business is whether or not to do it. Finding the perfect location runs a close second. Because all espresso businesses are essentially retail operations, accessing the customers who will support your business is crucial. You won't survive without them.

Securing that ideal location requires a great deal of thought and planning, and can be broken down into three basic steps: (1) establishing the criteria for analyzing the location; (2) hitting the pavement to find it; and (3) preparing and delivering a proposal to the landlord.

Establishing the Criteria for Accurate Analysis

Establishing an apt set of criteria before launching your location search is an indispensable part of finding a successful site for your business. Without a clear understanding of what you're looking for, you'll probably never find it.

If you have invested in the process of building a solid business plan, you're in good shape; the fundamentals are identified. Let your business plan guide the process. Did you pinpoint that you'd like to be open seven days a week, and employ four other people? Discover you want the autonomy and moderate scale of a one-person operation? In either case, the volume, scale, structure, and schedule you picture for yourself should be used as a vision against which each potential location is measured.

CUSTOMER BASE

All espresso operations, regardless of form, require a stable market from which to draw. This market may consist of students on the way to class, grocery shoppers, or fine diners, but in all cases it must be dependable and open to the concept of espresso.

Stake out a potential location and count customers. Talk to neighboring businesses to pick up on buying trends, busy days, peak hours, and general traffic flow. Spend time in operations similar to the one you intend to open, and evaluate the clientele of those who have succeeded.

If you're considering a drive-through, count cars. The city department of engineering or transportation may have traffic statistics on specific intersections. In a restaurant, take a look at your ticket items and see how many people are ordering desserts or after-dinner drinks.

Estimating an acceptable number of potential drinks is difficult, and depends on your goals for the business. Start with this maxim: one cart selling espresso as its primary product needs to sell an average minimum of 250 cups a day to survive.

Don't settle for less than you think you need; chances are, less is exactly what you'll get. Rather than assuming that each passerby is a potential cup of coffee, synthesize body count with an evaluation of the coffee culture potential in a given area. Again, who will your customers be? Will they keep you in business the way you envision?

VISIBILITY AND CONVENIENCE

Good visibility and easy access are strategic benefits. The more consumers who know your product is there—and can easily get to it—the better.

For some operations, such as the drive-through, exposure will be your primary method of marketing. Consider it carefully. When does the site first come into a motorist's view? Is it on the right side of the road for morning commuters? In general, people don't like obstacles. Don't count on anyone who has to make a left turn across traffic.

Once a customer spies your operation, she has to be able to reach it. What means of transportation will most customers use? Will it be a simple matter to park the car, hop off the bus, or walk across the intersection?

In a retail setting, make sure espresso machine placement suits the purpose you intend. If espresso is intended to function as a "draw," make it obvious to customers inside and outside the store. If you are part of a larger food service operation and your goal is to serve hospital staff, don't put the espresso machine by the front walk. Set up in the employee lounge or cafeteria.

AMBIANCE AND EXPOSURE TO THE ELEMENTS

The general atmosphere of your operation should be appealing for both you and your customers. If you don't like to hang around the place, no one else will, either. Particularly if you're planning a mobile-type operation, make sure the physical location will be comfortable, not just tolerable. Do you want to be indoors or outside? Will the location afford adequate protection against wind, rain, and cold? Someone—probably you—is going to have to stand there for twelve hours at a stretch, weather notwithstanding. Plan for space heaters, secure, watertight awnings, and anything else you need.

Where customers are concerned, outdoor tables during warm weather are a big plus. But these shouldn't be the only seating option if you want "for-here" business to be significant.

COMPETITION

Some competition is good. If there are no other espresso outfits in the area, it may mean that consumers aren't espresso-savvy. On the other hand, you know what they say about too much of a good thing. Ultimately, you'll have to judge this one on the basis of your experience, information gathering, and intuition.

HOURS OF OPERATION

It's important not only that the market exists, but that it flows during hours that are feasible for your business to be up and running. After you identify your market, figure out when customer traffic is likely to be the heaviest. During commuting hours? At intermission or half-time? On weekends? Make sure these are hours you're willing and able to be operational.

LOGISTICS AND TECHNICAL SPECIFICATIONS

Bear operations logistics in mind, especially if you're introducing espresso into a pre-existing retail or food service environment. Where are you going to put the espresso machine? Will the operator have ready access to the refrigerator, grinder, dump box, and service area? Who is the operator going to be?

In a takeout situation, if at all possible, put the espresso machine on the front counter so that the operator faces customers. This hides the messiest part of the operation. Such placement also prevents the operator from having to turn her back on her customers. She can maintain visual and verbal contact while preparing drinks. The espresso machine, itself an eye-catcher, will do some of your advertising for you.

Take future storage needs into account. No one can fit all of their inventory under the bed. Plan to have space for cases of hot cups, syrups, whole beans, and more. Make sure you have adequate storage space for the cart itself, in the commissary if that is required, or elsewhere. If your structure is a more permanent kiosk, make sure it can be secured, valuables inside, like a fortress.

If the following features are not already in place, make sure you are allowed to add them—and can afford to. For the espresso machine, you'll need 220-volt electricity. In most cases, you'll want extra outlets for the refrigerator, grinder, and drip brewer, as well as access to a water source (either plumbed in or available for tank refill).

LICENSING REQUIREMENTS AND THE COMMISSARY

Permit and licensing regulations are strict, and vary from region to region. Check these out ahead of time, and make required features a prominent part of your selection criteria. In general, licensing requirements may include a commissary (see separate discussion below), a predetermined number of sinks and water taps, adequate garbage facilities, and appropriate storage space for all foodstuffs.

If you are adding espresso to a location already licensed as a food service, generally all you'll have to do is make sure the equipment you choose carries up-to-date regulatory approvals and is installed to electrical, plumbing, and building codes.

In a noncoffee retail environment, you'll need to become a sort of mini-restaurant. You'll be obliged to meet the same requirements a restaurant does to gain health department approval. Don't let this scare you off: in most cases, it means installing the right number of sinks and making sure all the equipment used has the necessary regulatory approvals.

The sinks, usually two or three, are for utensil cleaning and hygiene purposes. You may have to make a fair investment in plumbing and electrical hookups. Almost always, however, the profit you reap justifies these improvements.

The health department requires that every mobile food service—a cart, a kiosk, a concessions or catering operation, or a drive-through classified as mobile—operate with a commissary. The need for a commissary is often overlooked, with disastrously expensive consequences, by newcomers to the industry.

According to the Second College Edition of *Webster's New World Dictionary*, "commissary" originally referred to the army officer in charge of providing soldiers with food and other supplies. Where your espresso operation is concerned, the commissary is the place where you clean and store your cart, wash utensils, service equipment, and sanitize everything.

The commissary may be a licensed restaurant or legally permitted church kitchen that you have gained permission to use. It may also be a structure you build yourself that meets all health department requirements. The specifications for a permittable commissary differ from place to place. To paint a general picture, these rules may be as follows:

- The commissary must provide adequate storage—including refrigeration when necessary—for all supplies.

- At the very least, plumbing must include a three-compartment sink, a mop sink, and a hand sink.

- The commissary must provide adequate facilities and space for storage and sanitation of all equipment, utensils, water tanks, and the cart.

- As a cart operator, you must have access to the commissary during all hours of business operation.

- Structurally, the commissary must have overhead protection, cleanable floors, a finish on walls and ceilings that meets code requirements, a fresh water source, and wastewater disposal facilities.

When planning your commissary site, don't overlook the basics: how wide is the entrance, and will you be able to get the cart in and out with ease? Is there space for shelving, to keep supplies up off the floor?

Be open to paying for the privilege of using a nearby restaurant as your commissary. Alternatively, building your own commissary is a good long-term investment. A "custom commissary" puts the fulfillment of health department requirements in your own hands, gives you that much more permanence in the eyes of your landlord, and provides a good base for future expansion. Begin with a size that is practical for your start-up operation, but think big. Five years from today, you may house an entire fleet of carts within the commissary walls.

Now that you've got a good idea of what to look for, it's time to design a set of criteria that will identify the ideal locations for your cart. Using the sample location criteria worksheet that follows as a guide, formulate your own. Then apply it.

Basic Commissary Floorplan

This basic floorplan is an example of a working commissary. Again: check with your local health department about applicable commissary requirements. You can't be too careful. If you find yourself unclear about any of the specifications, ask.

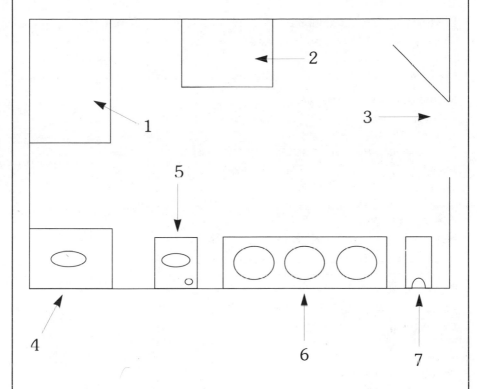

1–Storage shelves

2–NSF-approved reach-in refrigerator

3–Entry (40" wide)

4–Mop sink

5–Hand sink and soap dispenser

6–NSF-approved 3-compartment sink

7–Spigot

Sample Location Criteria Worksheet

NAME OF LOCATION: _____

ADDRESS: _____

PHONE: _____

CONTACT PERSON: _____

CUSTOMER BASE:

Foot traffic _____ Commuters _____ Local workers _____ Shoppers _____
Customers of neighboring businesses _____ Event attendees _____

PEAK TIMES, DAYS: _____

SITE VISIBILITY TO CUSTOMER BASE:

Excellent   Good   Fair   Poor

CONVENIENCE AND EASE OF ACCESS FOR CUSTOMER BASE:

Excellent   Good   Fair   Poor
Parking available?   Y/N

OPERATING HOURS:

Number of days per week necessary for full-service operation:
Hours of operation: _____ a.m./p.m. to _____ a.m./p.m.

COMPETITION:

Heavy   Moderate   Light   Nonexistent
Comments: _____
_____

FACILITY EVALUATION:

Indoor/outdoor _____ Protection from elements (if outdoor) _____
Electrical access _____ Storage for supplies/cart _____ Seating? _____

COMMISSARY POSSIBILITIES, IF NECESSARY:

1.

2.

3.

NOTES:

(*Useful notes might include information about visual marketing
opportunities (sandwich board, office park registry, marquis), co-
promotions (with a movie theatre, for example), and so on.*)

Evaluating Sites

As the introduction to this book points out, people are introducing espresso just about everywhere. Use your imagination to come up with sites, and use the criteria you've just established. Just like an exam, you're going to have to grade the locations you find to see if they "pass." Take the time to work through each aspect of a potential site. Be honest with yourself, and don't be afraid to deliberate. Hasty decisions could cost a great deal of money and wasted effort.

The more sophisticated your plans, the more sense it makes to seek outside help. There are professional leasing agents who specialize in busy corners. There are others who specialize in outside seating, office buildings, and strip malls. If you're in a reasonably saturated espresso market and worried about securing a good spot, you may want to consult one of these professionals.

Early in the development of a market, however, securing a profitable location yourself is eminently doable. Here are a few general site suggestions to help you get started:

- hospital or medical center
- courthouse or other municipal building
- university campus
- pre-existing retail store (office products, toy store)
- park
- sporting arena
- gas station
- movie theater
- office building lobby
- car wash
- shopping mall
- strip mall
- bookstore
- defunct fast-food joint
- transit center
- bus stop
- train station
- airport
- busy sidewalk
- library
- street corner
- convention center
- "superstore"
- grocery store
- performance hall
- professional building
- hair salon
- art gallery
- gym
- vacant lot

After you have walked through this systematic process of elimination, identifying the specific locations that will support the booming espresso business you intend to run, you're ready to move on to the next step: proposing to the landlords.

Preparing a Winning Proposal for the Landlord

What you gain by preparing a well-written, nicely presented proposal is this: you separate yourself out from the other espresso business hopefuls who are walking around, knocking on doors and chatting up landowners.

In addition, by submitting this handsome, well-thought-out piece of work, you are giving your potential landlord all the information she needs to make a decision in your favor. While you're not forcing her to produce an answer on the spot (which will often work to your detriment, particularly if the concept of an espresso operation is a new one), the decision maker has everything necessary, in black and white, to allay her fears.

In most cases, the delivery or presentation of your proposal to a landlord will be your first contact with her. Don't underestimate the impact of this meeting. Again, your overall objective is to convince the landlord that having your attractive, popular espresso operation around will be of great benefit.

Most landlords aren't keen on taking risks with their property, so try and pay particular attention to addressing concerns from their point of view. Put yourself in the decision maker's shoes. What concerns would you have? The more information you can furnish up front, the more likely the landlord will be to feel comfortable with your idea.

Your proposal should include the following information:

- **What is the business concept?** This section should function as an overall operating description.

- **What's it going to look like?** Pictures, drawings, or photos, which you may be able to get from suppliers or have an artist or illustrator draw up for you, work well here. Make your vision tangible.

- **Will the espresso business add to or detract from the current value of the location?** Detail the ways in which you believe your operation will add to the value of the site.

- **What kind of a following is this venture going to attract?** And will it increase customer volume for the landlord or other tenants?

- **What will you be serving?** Include a menu, nicely typeset with logo—even if you don't yet have your business up and going.

- Last, but not least, every landlord wants to know: *What's in it for me?*

This final question is probably the most important of the bunch. Gear your presentation toward the specific location in question, and what you have to offer. Let the landlord know your presence will enhance her location. Persuasive points might include customer service (because the espresso service is there as a unique benefit to consumers), and an accompanying increase in the appeal of the location. Planned leasehold improvements contribute to value as well.

Then there's rent. Consider not including a firm rent figure in your initial proposal. Rather than considering your proposal as an "offer," think of it as a tool to open the doors for discussion. If the decision maker becomes sold on the benefits of the idea, you may be able to negotiate a spontaneous arrangement that works to your advantage—a moderate fixed fee, perhaps. Another option, seen frequently among cart, kiosk, and concessions operators, is to agree to pay a percentage of monthly gross sales.

Rent agreements go all over the board. They may be as little as nothing, in which case the landlord feels that she is gaining just by offering your service to customers. On the other hand, in some rare cases, rent may amount to as much as 35–40% of sales. You should be willing to pay rent, even if you're a "mobile" operation like a cart or concession. Your access to the location, regardless of the service you're prepared to provide, is a privilege.

If you are the first entrepreneur to propose this kind of idea to the landlord, let her know that once the market gets active—and it will—the fact that she already has an espresso service will set her property apart. Write a few paragraphs describing the espresso business itself, a bit of history focusing on the rapid growth of espresso in the Seattle area, how espresso is one key facet of the swiftly expanding specialty coffee industry. Present your proposal as an opportunity for collaboration in the local pioneering of this unique and successful business.

Remember that forethought and a professional presentation will set you apart. Some enterprising individuals even go to the length of having a professional artist draw a picture of their operation, cheerful and prosperous, doing business in the proposed location. This gives the decision maker quite a clear idea of what the espresso business will look like, and how it will fit in with her business or property. The cost for such an illustration may range from $50 to $500. Only you can decide if the investment is worthwhile.

Leave your materials with the landlord, and make plans to follow up at a later date. Forcing an instant decision will almost always work against you. The decision maker will feel put on the spot and, if she feels even the slightest uncertainty about your proposal, will respond with a NO.

Allow some time for your prospective landlord to internalize the data. Represent yourself well, be persuasive, and—ultimately—trust in the process.

One last piece of advice: submit no fewer than five proposals at the same time. Odds are that at least one of the five will be accepted. If you "win" with more than one, so much the better. You are then in a position to choose the arrangement that works best for you. At the same time, you have succeeded in opening doors for the future expansion of your business.

Negotiating the Lease

The function of your proposal was to open the door for negotiation. Once your prospective landlord has reviewed the proposal, both of you are ready to take the next step.

There are scores and scores of books written about the fine points of negotiating a good lease, and if you're new to this you may want to consult one. In addition, these general guidelines will dramatically increase your chances of success:

- Keep an open mind.

- Make sure your proposal is open-ended enough to allow for negotiation.

- Remember that your landlord doesn't have to choose you, or choose to host an espresso operation at all. He was humming along just fine before you decided to go into the business. Make both the process, and the prospect, of having you around as attractive as possible.

- Create a win-win situation for both parties.

On the pages that follow, you'll find a sample landlord proposal and a sample lease, both of which will help you prepare for your own presentations and negotiations.

Sample Landlord Proposal

The following proposal was originally written for a cart located near the front entrance of a grocery store. The majority of its components, however, apply to all of the business concepts discussed in this book and can easily be modified for use with any of them.

PROPOSAL TO GROCERY STORE

Joe Monaghan, dba Mocha Joe's, proposes to the Grocery Store to operate an espresso coffee vending cart at or near the entrance of the grocery store No. 357 located at 1234 SE 22nd Street.

The contents of this proposal are as follows:

1. General Description of the Business
The Company
The Concept
Facilities
Management
Proposed Remuneration (Rent)
Proposed Hours of Operation
Proposed Date of Opening

2. Physical Requirements
Operating Space
Electrical
Use of Commissary
Storage

3. Benefits to the Grocery Store
Customer Service
Additional Foot Traffic
Additional Revenue
Enhanced Image
Co-Promotions
Enhanced Sense of Community

4. Examples of Similar Operations

5. Exhibits
Sample Menu
Site Plan
Cart Photo

1. General Description of the Business

THE COMPANY

Mocha Joe's Espresso was established in June of 1990 by Joe and Denise Monaghan to build a fleet of espresso vending carts in and around the Seattle area. Currently, Mocha Joe's Espresso includes four cart operations, along with a successful espresso catering and special events division. All units, as well as the catering and special events division, are operating at a profitable level. In the company's original business plan, Mocha Joe's forecasted and committed to an expansion rate of one additional cart per year. A list of current locations and references is available upon request.

THE CONCEPT

It is the intent of Mocha Joe's to provide high-quality espresso coffee drinks, served and prepared individually, using the highest quality ingredients (see Menu). We are certain that the Grocery Store is well aware of the growth in popularity of espresso drinks and that grocery supermarkets have been home to several such operations. It has been our observation that these types of operations have been considerably more successful when owner operated. It is our intent to complement the store with an attractive and upscale image along with an energetic atmosphere.

After conducting extensive market research, we chose the Grocery Store as an excellent potential location for the following reasons:

1. High Traffic
2. Lack of Competition
3. Excellent Demographics

We are aware that there are some plans to remodel your particular store, and that the possibility exists for espresso to be served "in house." It is our hope to convince the Grocery Store that all parties involved would gain by choosing to subcontract this particular part of the business to us.

Our research shows that a cart operating out in front of a store typically generates a significantly higher volume of sales than an espresso machine placed in a department of the store such as the deli or bakery. In addition, the preparation of excellent espresso drinks requires a certain amount of expertise and genuine dedication. We, as owner operators, would be in a position to maintain high quality standards which will result in higher revenues to ourselves and to the Grocery Store.

FACILITIES

Mocha Joe's will make use of the finest equipment available to facilitate the operation of business. Our self-contained espresso cart is equipped with a fresh water system, hot and cold running water, a hand sink, a refrigerator, and a full breakered electrical system to ensure safety and sanitation as well as meet all existing codes and regulations. Externally, the cart is made of attractive, top-of-the-line materials. Colors and graphics have been carefully chosen so as to maintain a clean, professional image (see photo in Exhibits).

MANAGEMENT
The proposed operation will be owned and operated by Joe Monaghan. It is my intent to maintain superb quality standards by operating the cart personally until a significant customer base has been established. When deemed appropriate, employees of Mocha Joe's will be hired based on the highest of standards and thoroughly trained in operations and customer service. In addition, we have retained the services of Julie Huffaker, a local consultant to the espresso industry, for training and industry insights.

PROPOSED REMUNERATION (RENT)
Mocha Joe's proposes to pay the Grocery Store a monthly rent of $250.00 or 7% of monthly gross sales, whichever is greater. Our projections put sales to average $6,000 to $9,000 per month within 6 months of opening.

PROPOSED HOURS OF OPERATION
    Mon–Sat   7:00 a.m. to 7:00 p.m.
    Sun   7:00 a.m. to 5:00 p.m.

PROPOSED DATE OF OPENING
    Approximately March 15, 1994

2. Physical Requirements

OPERATING SPACE
    Approximately 50 sq. feet (5' x 10')

ELECTRICAL
    220 volt, 30 amp circuit. NEMA L14-30

It is understood that Mocha Joe's will be responsible for any costs associated with the installation of the electrical outlet.

USE OF EXISTING FACILITY AS COMMISSARY
The County Health Department requires all espresso carts to secure the use of a "licensed kitchen" to serve as a commissary for clean-up area. Use of the facility consists of the washing of a few utensils and the filling of water tanks and should pose no problem to the staff of the existing operation.

STORAGE

There is a need for minimal storage (approximately 20 cu. ft.) for inventory and supplies. In addition, access to a moderate amount of refrigeration or the space for a small, personally owned refrigerator is necessary. The cart itself can be secured, folded, and covered to facilitate easy storage.

3. Benefits to the Grocery Store

CUSTOMER SERVICE

We will be offering high quality products that are in high demand but not currently offered to the Grocery Store's customers.

ADDITIONAL FOOT TRAFFIC

Similar business concepts placed at grocery stores and other retailers have shown that the espresso carts can generate foot traffic, as many customers make a daily stop at the cart.

ADDITIONAL REVENUE

It is our intent to purchase as many supplies as possible from the store such as milk, sweeteners, and baked goods (if applicable).

ENHANCED IMAGE

The Mocha Joe's operation will aid the Grocery Store's public relations efforts effectively and without cost.

CO-PROMOTIONS

Mocha Joe's is willing and anxious to participate in any co-promotions with the Grocery Store that will be of mutual benefit.

ENHANCED SENSE OF COMMUNITY

Mocha Joe's primary market will be the surrounding neighborhood. It is common for many espresso consumers to make a daily stop at their favorite espresso bar. Many people would appreciate this type of service being available in their community.

4. Examples of Similar Operations

Below is a list of independently owned and operated espresso carts that are located at grocery supermarkets in the Seattle area:

1. *(fill in your own!)*
2.
3.
4.

5. Exhibits

SAMPLE ESPRESSO MENU

	1 oz.	2 oz.
ESPRESSO	$1.00	$1.50

Strong, intense brew served straight

	8 oz.	12 oz.	16 oz.
CAFFE LATTE	$1.35	$1.65	$1.95

Espresso and steamed milk, topped with froth

CAPPUCCINO	$1.35	$1.65	$1.95

Espresso with equal parts steamed and frothed milk

CAFFE MOCHA	$1.60	$1.90	$2.20

Espresso with steamed hot chocolate, topped with whipped cream

Flavors (in any drink)   add $0.25
Almond, Hazelnut, Vanilla

Double Shot (in any drink)   add $0.50

Pastries baked fresh daily • Prices and selection vary

SITE PLAN

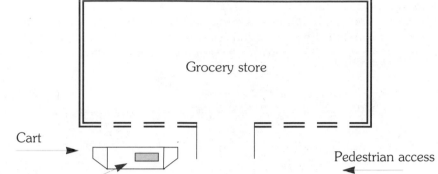

Grocery store

Cart

Espresso machine

Pedestrian access

Customer parking

CART PHOTOGRAPH

Illustration courtesy of Monaco Espresso;
photograph by Kim Morton

Sample Lease

The primary purpose of the sample lease that follows is to provide a representation of all or part of necessary lease content. Although, if properly signed by mutually agreeing parties, it would be a legally binding document, it is strongly recommended that both parties seek competent legal counsel prior to entering into any agreement.

This lease made this _____ day of _____ , 19 _____ , by and between (Names & Addresses) _____

_____

(hereinafter called Lessor) and _____

_____

(hereinafter called Lessee).

Witnesseth:

1. PREMISES: Lessor does hereby lease to Lessee, those certain premises commonly known as

as shown on Exhibit A (if necessary).

2. USE: Lessee shall have use of leased premises, for the placement and operation of an espresso cart or kiosk, as physically described and depicted on Exhibit B.

3. PRODUCTS & EXCLUSIVE RIGHTS TO SELL: Lessor shall grant to Lessee the exclusive right to the sale of espresso coffee beverages, gourmet brewed coffee beverages, and granita products. Lessor shall prohibit the sale of these products by any other vendors on the above described premises.

4. RENT: Lessee agrees to pay Lessor rent in the amount of $ ____ per month, or ____ % of the monthly gross sales of the cart, whichever is greater.

5. TERM: This lease shall commence on the ____ day of ____ , 19 ____ , and last for a period of ____ years from that date. Lessee shall have the right to renew the lease for an additional ____ years providing all terms of the agreement have been met.

6. COMMISSARY: Lessor will make available the facility described as for the use as a commissary to meet health department requirements, and to properly clean and maintain the operation.

7. STORAGE: Lessor agrees to provide Lessee with ____ square feet of dry storage space within reasonable distance from the cart operating site.

8. ELECTRICAL INSTALLATION: Lessee, at his/her own cost, will have the right to install a ____ volt, ____ amp, electrical circuit and receptacle within ____ feet of the cart operating site. Lessee will use a qualified and licensed contractor for the installation of the circuit and receptacle.

9. UTILITIES: Lessor shall pay the cost of the use of electricity and water necessary for the operation of the espresso cart.

10. ASSIGNMENT: Lessee shall not sublet the whole or any part of the Premises nor assign this lease without the prior written consent of Lessor. Lessor shall not unreasonably withhold consent of assignment, providing proposed assignee has demonstrated operational ability, including proper training by Lessee.

11. SIGNS AND ALTERATIONS: All signs placed upon premises, and any alterations to premises, shall require the prior written consent of Lessor.

12. PERMITS AND LICENSES: Lessee will obtain all necessary federal, state, and local licenses and permits, prior to the opening of the espresso cart operation.

13. ACCIDENTS, LIABILITY, & INSURANCE: Lessee agrees to hold Lessor harmless from any claim, action, and/or judgment arising out of the activities of Lessee on the Premises, unless caused by Lessor's negligence. Lessee agrees to procure and maintain business liability insurance in the amount of $1,000,000.00 (one million dollars). Lessor shall not be liable for damage, destruction or theft of any of Lessee's property unless caused by Lessor's negligence.

14. NOTICES: Any notices required to be given by either party to the other shall be delivered by U.S. Postal Service, or other commercial delivery or courier service, postage or delivery costs prepaid, addressed to the following addresses:

Lessor   Lessee

_____   _____

_____   _____

_____   _____

_____   _____

Either party shall give other party 30 days advanced, written notice of change of address.

IN WITNESS WHEREOF, the parties hereto have hereunto set their hands and seals this _____ day of _____ , 19 _____ .

Lessor(s)   Lessee(s)

_____   _____
_____   _____
_____   _____
_____   _____

Checklist: Landing the Location

____ **Establish criteria and create worksheet for location analysis, including:**

    ____ Site name and contact information

    ____ Customer base

    ____ Peak times, days

    ____ Site visibility

    ____ Convenience and ease of access

    ____ Operating hours

    ____ Competition

    ____ Technical specifications and licensing issues

    ____ Other

____ **Identify potential sites**

    ____ Identify promising locations

    ____ Use location criteria worksheet to evaluate them

    ____ Decide which sites are viable

____ **Write proposals to landlords, including:**

    ____ Description of the business concept

    ____ Pictures or drawings of what you propose

    ____ Explanation of how it will add value to the location

    ____ Description of who will patronize the new business

    ____ Description of what you will serve

    ____ Explanation of benefits to the landlord

____ **Submit proposals and follow up**

____ **Negotiate and sign lease**

CHAPTER 4
Permits and Licensing

Do your homework up front. Before you go out and spend any money for equipment or renovations, get a clear idea of what's going to be required for your business in the way of permits and licensing, by whom, and exactly what you're going to need to fulfill those requirements. Licensing requirements will affect the way you manage your expenses, the location you choose, and the equipment you select. You can spare significant time and financial resources by researching all requirements carefully, and proceeding with a patient and generous attitude.

There are two general categories of permits and licensing of which the new espresso entrepreneur should be acutely aware: business and health. Business permitting is standard for any entrepreneurial undertaking. The health department considerations associated with setting up an espresso business are specific to the food service industry and can prove quite involved.

City and State Business Licenses, Federal Tax ID Number

Licensing requirements differ from city to city, state to state. Depending on your experience in business, you may want to use this section as a refresher, a reminder, or a starting point. In any case, be sure to cover all the bases—state, city, and federal—by carefully researching the regulations particular to your area. It's far better not to have any surprises.

City

To find out about city licensing, go down to City Hall! City licenses are fairly straightforward, most often applying to those enterprises that do business within the city limits. This licensing is a simple process, usually renewable on an annual basis and demanding a relatively low fee.

State

Most states have a state business licensing program. State licenses are easy to get, with fees ranging from $25.00 on up. A quick phone call to the state department of revenue (check your state government blue pages) will get the application process started. Upon receiving a completed application, the state will assign the "tax-paying ID number" with which your business will forever be identified.

Federal

Although a federal tax ID number is not crucial unless you're planning to hire employees, it's still a good idea to have one right from the start. You'll probably save yourself the trouble later on down the line. Pick up the phone and give the closest IRS office a call (try the federal government blue pages for a toll-free option). An official will mail you the appropriate forms and phone numbers. Getting that federal ID number is an easy process, and doesn't cost a thing.

Health Department Regulations and Submitting a "Plan Review"

Regardless of the form your business takes, you're probably going to have to deal with the health department in one form or other. The only exception is when you've already secured permits for a food service to which you intend to add espresso.

Winning the blessing of the health department is one of the most critical elements to getting a good start with your espresso business. This process can be either easy and smooth or frustratingly drawn out, depending both on the thoroughness of the information you present and the espresso-specific knowledge and experience of the health department officials themselves.

WHICH CODES APPLY?

One of the earliest steps in your business planning should be to call the local health department and find out what health codes apply to your venture. Be prepared, during this conversation, to give a basic description of your business. Do you already have some sort of permit? What items are you planning to serve? Name the specific equipment you'll be using. Even if you can't furnish exact brand names at this point, at least name each separate piece. The health official will be able to tell you if regulatory approvals—Underwriter's Laboratory (UL) or National Sanitation Foundation (NSF), for example—are necessary for any individual item.

Obtain an official copy of the governing codes appropriate to your business and when you have them in hand, read carefully. Look closely for required items, commissary regulations, and any particulars you might not have expected. If you're planning to open an espresso cart, you may find that there are not yet codes in your area that apply. It may well become your job to educate the health department about espresso. Educating them *well* is certainly in your best interests.

Consider writing for a copy of the Seattle/King County, Washington health codes for "mobile food services," and offer local officials a copy to use as a model. This set of regulations is among the most comprehensive in the country. Even if all the codes won't ultimately apply to your case, you may want to be proactive and inspire the confidence of your health department by taking them on.

If you are planning to do special events catering, you may be able to get by without a mobile food service permit. In many areas, the health department's physical requirements for catering are much less than for regular mobile operations. If your event locations have adequate facilities (again, check with the health department for restrictions), individual vendors only need "temporary health permits." The promoter of the event can give you advice about how to obtain one.

You may also want to consider structuring an arrangement in which you are subcontracting through another catering company. If you sell your services through them, and they are appropriately permitted, you may not need your own permit.

SUBMITTING A PLAN REVIEW

Almost any time you need to obtain a new license from the health department, you must submit a plan review. Health departments may not always call it this, or in fact require one, but a plan review is always appreciated and will further your success during the permitting process.

So what exactly is this plan review? It is a written document, packed with information about your business. Its standard format is part application, part operating summary. With a plan review, you are communicating to the health department precisely what you have in mind for your proposed business. Especially if espresso is new to your market, a detailed plan review will embolden health department officials to allow you take the lead.

The basic steps for preparing this plan review are similar from market to market and operation to operation; specific content, however, will vary. The plan review for a retail coffee business, for example, may need to include information about the floor finish, wall finishes, and where all sinks are located. The plan review for an espresso cart might need details about the location and facilities of the commissary.

Approach the composition of your plan review with logic and clarity. The health department doesn't want any surprises, and you will be more successful when there aren't any.

A good plan review consists of these basic elements:

1. A drawing or design of your espresso setup. This is necessary to reassure the assigned health department official that your equipment and protocol will comply faithfully with all requirements, and cause no problems. Hiring a professional architect or designer to whip up a structural diagram is not necessary, but do make the diagrams clear. The easier they are to read, the smoother the overall process will be.

The drawing should include top, front, and side views of the entire espresso station. Equipment layout should be represented in detail. Show where the espresso machine goes, on which counter the grinder sits, and so on. Include your pastry case, if applicable; don't forget condiment containers, the cash register—everything. The health department official should be able to gain a good idea on paper of how your business will look on the counter or sidewalk.

2. All the information and specifications you have about equipment involved in hand washing. Specify the type of tanks, heater, and drain you'll be using. Show precisely how the water lines and drain will run, and exactly where the drain container will sit.

3. A thorough description of business operations. This should cover everything included in the day-to-day operation of your espresso business: a detailed menu, the items (and their ingredients) featured, preparation procedures for each of those items, and all of your operating procedures.

Describe setup, the opening and initial cleaning of the espresso station, operations during the business day (including ongoing cleaning and proper rotation of utensils), and closing procedures. Closing procedures for a cart, for example, might include the cart's return to the commissary, the washing of utensils in your three-compartment sink, the cleaning of the cart itself, and the retiring of supplies—milk, cups, etc.

Again, the Seattle/King County plan review outline provides an excellent example of what to include. These guidelines, along with a sample plan review and a checklist for completing all the necessary permitting steps, are included on the pages that follow.

A FINAL WORD ABOUT THE HEALTH DEPARTMENT

Educating health department officials can be a very positive process. The worst thing for everyone, and certainly for you, is to develop an antagonistic relationship with the department. Don't look at the health department official as your adversary. Have respect for his position. This official is part of a larger bureaucracy, and is simply trying to do his job in a responsible way.

Ultimately, you may have to convince the health department that you can't, or won't, comply with some requirements. (We mention this at the latter part of the chapter because most espresso operators find it tempting to throw in the towel and refuse compliance at a very early stage.) Experience shows that the good will engendered by doing your best to follow the rules will pay off in the long run. If the health department has the impression that you are generally cooperative, they may cut you some slack when it counts.

Sample Mobile Food Service Plan Review Outline (Seattle/King County)

The following sample plan review outline and plan review should give you a good feel for what might be required by your local health department, and in what format. However, don't stop here! Check with health department officials in your area for the precise parameters you will be expected to meet.

The Seattle/King County Health Department Advises:

Use the following guidelines to assure that you have included all necessary information. If you have questions, please call your local plans examiner.

When submitting, it is important to make sure your plans are clear and easy to read, that you have provided three copies of all documents, and that you have included the nonrefundable Plan Review Fee ($200.00 for all King County operators).

Plans should be put together in the following order:

1. COVER PAGE
   - Name of mobile food service.
   - Address where the cart will be located. Include zip code.
   - The contact person's name, address, and phone number.

2. ITEMIZED MENU
   - List the food you will be serving. Include condiments, iced beverages, the sources of food not made by you, and packaging details.

3. A TOP DRAWING OF THE CART/VEHICLE/STRUCTURE
   - Dimensions.
   - Layout of all equipment and supplies. Include cash register, hand soap and paper towels, knock boxes, espresso machines, hot dog cookers, condiments, baked goods, etc.

4. AN OPERATOR'S SIDE VIEW OF THE CART OR ELEVATIONS OF THE VEHICLE
   - Dimensions.
   - Layout of all equipment.
   - Cold holding equipment. Make and model of refrigerator. In most cases, commercial refrigeration is required.
   - Finishes on surfaces.

5. A Drawing of the Water System

- Spec sheet on the hot water heater. (The page that indicates the hot water heater has an adjustable thermostat.)
- Size and material of the fresh water and waste water tanks. Hand sink must have at least 5 gallons fresh water. Waste tank needs to be 15% larger than fresh water tank. If additional water is needed, such as for espresso, show additional supply.
- Type of pump.
- Tubing material. Must be drinking-water approved.
- Waste connection. Must be either tight fitting with a quick disconnect or tight plumbed.
- General idea of how the water system fits on the mobile unit.

6. Side View

- Dimensions.

7. Front View

- Dimensions.
- Indicate overhead protection.

8. Commissary Details

- Letter from owner of the commissary if you are using someone else's approved kitchen. Letter must indicate you have access to dish washing, refrigeration, and storage at the time(s) you have indicated you will be using it.
- Detailed plans for commissary layout if you are building your own.
- Distance of commissary from operating site.

9. Rest Room Availability Letter

- Letter/lease giving permission for mobile operators to use rest rooms.

10. Site Map

- Location of mobile food service operation.
- Location of cart storage.
- For single locations, include location of commissary and rest rooms.
- For routes, include details of all stops and time at stops.

11. Operating Procedures

- Hours of operation.
- Time at commissary.

- How and where water tanks will be filled.
- How and where waste water tanks will be emptied.
- Cleaning during the day.
- Cleaning at the commissary.
- Details of any food preparation.

12. CONCLUDE WITH:

"NO CHANGES WILL BE MADE WITHOUT HEALTH DEPARTMENT APPROVAL."

Mobile Food Service Plan Review Outline reprinted courtesy of the Seattle/King County Health Department.

Sample Plan Review for Mobile Food Service

For:

Joe Monaghan
Owner of Mocha Joe's Espresso
108 SE Summer St.
Seattle, WA 98102
(206) 555-1234

Proposed Espresso Cart Locations:

Grocery Store No. 372
1234 SE 22nd Street
Seattle, WA 98112

Proposed Commissary Locations:

On site at each location

Table of Contents:

Menu
Food Storage and Dispensing Methods
Operational Procedures: Opening, Ongoing, Closing, and Hours
Site Plan
Cart Plans and Specs

Menu

1. Espresso (1-ounce servings of espresso coffee, served "straight")

2. Caffe Latte (espresso with steamed milk)

3. Cappuccino (espresso with foamed milk)

4. Caffe Mocha (espresso with steamed chocolate milk)

5. Flavored Caffe Latte (espresso with steamed milk and flavored syrup)

6. Condiments (cinnamon, vanilla powder, cocoa in shakers, sugar and artificial sweeteners in packets)

7. Assorted Pastries (to be purchased from wholesalers)

Explanation of Food Storage and Dispensing Methods

COFFEES

All coffees come packed in 5-lb. cellophane bags, containing whole beans. All coffees will be stored in their original containers at least 6 inches off the floor and protected from splash.

Upon order, ground coffee is dispensed directly from a coffee grinder into a filter/handle which is attached to the espresso machine. Hot water (195°F) is forced through the ground coffee directly into a paper cup.

Spent grounds are placed into a stainless steel dump box. This dump box will be emptied several times daily into a trash receptacle. All coffee is sold to go in single service disposable cups. Unused cups will be stored behind the Plexiglas sneeze-guard that is attached to the cart, or in prefabricated cup dispensers that are mounted in the cart.

STEAMED MILK

Steamed milk will be used in many of the espresso drinks. Milk will be delivered fresh on site and stored in the on-site refrigerator at 40°F or lower.

Upon order, the required amount of milk will be poured from the original container into a stainless steel pitcher. The container of milk is then returned to the refrigerator. The milk in the steaming pitcher is heated to approximately 170°F using the steaming attachment of the espresso machine and poured directly into the paper cup.

The steaming pitcher, along with any residual milk, is then immediately returned to the refrigerator. The nozzle of the steam attachment is immediately wiped with a cloth that has been dipped in sanitizing solution, and the cloth is returned to the solution.

FLAVORED SYRUPS

Some menu items involve the addition of flavored syrups. In such cases, the syrup will be poured directly from the original containers (25-oz. glass bottles) into the single service cup.

CONDIMENTS

Condiments consist of cinnamon, chocolate powder, vanilla powder, and cocoa powder and will be dispensed from shaker type canisters. Sugar and sugar substitutes will be provided in single serving paper packets.

PAPER PRODUCTS

All paper products will be stored in dispensers (napkins and straws) or in the original containers.

ICE

Ice will be kept in an ice chest. This ice chest will be used only for ice storage, and will be washed, rinsed, and sanitized daily at the commissary.

PASTRIES

All pastry products will be displayed in a Plexiglas display case and served individually using wax paper squares to avoid contact with the server's hand.

Operational Procedures

OPENING

Prior to opening, cart operator will perform the following steps:

1. Prepare sanitizing solution in a 1 gallon plastic bucket using chlorine bleach and hot water in a ratio of 1 teaspoon bleach to 1 gallon water to be used during operation.
2. Transfer milk from the commissary refrigerator to ice chest for carriage to the operational site. After the cart has been plugged in and the "on cart refrigerator" has reached temperature of less than 40°F, the milk will be transferred into the cart refrigerator.

3. Transfer adequate supply of other items (cups, coffee beans, and other paper products) from commissary to cart.
4. Fill water supply canisters with fresh water from approved water source (three compartment sink)
5. Transfer cart to operational site.

Total expected setup time is 30 minutes.

ONGOING CLEANING METHODS

During operation, all surfaces will be frequently wiped down with cloths dipped in sanitizing solution. An adequate supply of presanitized towels (6) will be kept in ziplock plastic bags to facilitate frequent turnover of soiled towels. Cart operators will wash hands frequently. A hand sink with hot running water, hand soap, and paper towels will be provided on the cart as well as in the commissary.

All milk products will be stored in the cart refrigerator at 40°F or lower.

An adequate supply of washed and sanitized milk steaming pitchers (4) will be used so as to allow replacement of used pitchers every 3 hours.

CLOSING AND CLEAN-UP

At the end of each working day, the cart operator will perform these steps:

1. Transfer milk from cart refrigerator to ice chest for transfer to commissary. Any residual milk in steaming pitchers will be discarded.
2. Disconnect cart from power supply and transfer cart to commissary for clean-up.

After reaching commissary:

1. Transfer milk from ice chest into commissary refrigerator.
2. Empty coffee dump box into trash can. Empty trash can into dumpster and rinse trash can.
3. Empty waste water into mop sink.
4. Prepare hot soapy water solution in sink compartment 1. Fill second compartment with hot rinse water. Fill third compartment with sanitizing solution (1/4 cup bleach per 5 gallons hot water). Thoroughly wash, rinse, and sanitize all utensils including milk steaming pitchers. Air dry all utensils in rack on sink drain board.
5. Completely wipe down cart surfaces and all equipment with cloth dipped in sanitizing solution.
6. Mop commissary floor and dispose of mop water in mop sink.

BUSINESS HOURS

9:00 a.m. to 9:00 p.m. daily

TIMES AT COMMISSARY

1/2 hour prior to opening and 1/2 hour after closing.

NO CHANGES MAY BE MADE WITHOUT PRIOR HEALTH DEPARTMENT APPROVAL.

SITE PLAN

Grocery store

Cart

Espresso machine

Pedestrian access

Customer parking

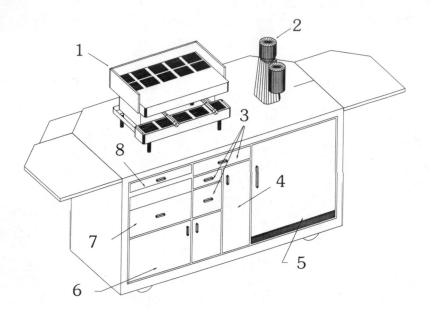

1. Espresso machine

2. Grinder

3. Drawers

4. Water tank

5. Refrigerator

6. Waste water tank

7. Enclosed sink

8. Cash drawer

Illustration courtesy of Monaco Espresso

CART SPECIFICATIONS

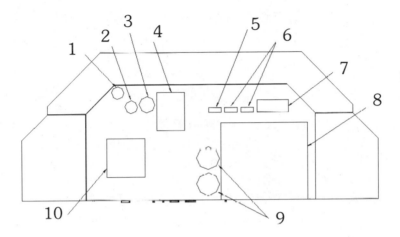

1. Water filter
2. Accumulator tank
3. Water pump
4. Water heater
5. 220 VAC outlet

6. 110 VAC outlets
7. 50 AMP sub-panel
8. Refrigerator
9. Water supply tanks
10. Sink

Illustration courtesy of Monaco Espresso

CART WATER SYSTEM

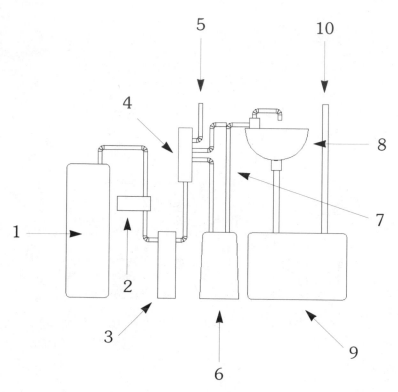

1. Water tank
2. Pump
3. Filter
4. Cold water
5. Water to espresso machine
6. Water heater
7. Hot water
8. Sink
9. Grey water holding tank
10. Drain from espresso machine

Checklist: Permits and Licensing

____ **Obtain City/County Business License**

    ____ Contact City Business Licensing Department

    ____ Request new business forms and applications

    ____ Complete and return with application fee(s)

____ **Obtain State Business License**

    ____ Contact Department of Revenue/ State Business Licensing Department

    ____ Request new business forms and applications

    ____ Complete and return with application fee(s)

____ **Obtain Federal Tax ID Number**

    ____ Contact local Internal Revenue Service office

    ____ Request application for Federal Taxpayer ID Number

    ____ Complete and return

____ **Apply for health permit**

    ____ Contact local health department

    ____ Describe business concept in detail

    ____ Request applicable codes and application forms

    ____ Determine requirements for specific concept, including:

        ____ Commissary

        ____ Sinks, drainage

        ____ Wall and floor finishes

        ____ Regulatory approvals (UL, ETL, NSF)

    ____ Prepare plan review, if necessary, being sure to include:

        ____ Business description

        ____ Site plan, drawings, specifications

        ____ Menu

        ____ Operational procedures

    ____ Complete these and any other necessary health permit applications, and return them with application fee(s)

    ____ Work with health department to make any required changes

CHAPTER 5
Financing Your
Espresso Venture

The bottom line, so to speak, is this: either you already have enough money to start your espresso business, or you're going to have to find it.

If you have ample funds in your own private or business reserve, one available option is to keep good records and jump right in. Even if you have the necessary capital, you may want to keep it in reserve and strategize a different route. But few people start out with all the necessary funding at their fingertips; most have to figure costs carefully, locate the appropriate financial resources, and then take the plunge.

The good news is that you can build a profitable business either way. But whether you are your only business partner or you have support from a lending source, charting the financial path of your business up front is well advised. Engage in a little realistic planning before you spend that first espresso dollar.

Calculating Costs

The most important part of this or any financing effort is knowing how much money you need. To get started, you'll have to draw up an opening budget.

Every foreseeable expense should be included. Add inventory and equipment, electrical appliances and hookup, signage and other marketing materials, snazzy uniforms, and training to your equation. Often overlooked—but potentially substantial—is the cost of operating before the business starts to pay for itself. The hope, of course, is that customers will line the sidewalk on opening day, but it's much safer to be conservative, and be prepared.

The start-up costs worksheet on the following page is designed to lead you through the process of enumerating these costs. Customize it to match your specific situation. We suggest reading through the entire book and making a list of applicable expenses *before* you actually sit down to fill in these blanks. If you count on remembering to add to the equation as you go along, you'll be more likely to leave something out.

Finding Funding

Once you know how much money you need to open and run your espresso operation, you have to figure out where to get it.

BANKS AND OTHER INSTITUTIONS

Typically, banks are most eager to lend money to those who need it the least. There are volumes written on how to present a bank loan proposal and if that is the route you choose, read a few. Check your local library, bookstore, the closest Small Business Administration (SBA) or Small Business Development office for resources.

There are some alternative sources. Community development groups, credit unions, and special interest agencies may have funds available. In addition to calling the SBA or Small Business Development office, contact your local Chamber of Commerce to find out about the lending potential of these organizations.

PRIVATE INVESTORS

There are other sources for financing. You can take on a business partner or partners, approach family members, or contract to borrow from friends. In all cases, your creditor will

Start-Up Costs Worksheet

This is an example of what you'll want to consider when figuring your own start-up costs. It is by no means all-inclusive; each individual business makes its own unique demands on the budget. Give careful consideration to the categories of costs yours will incur, and customize the list accordingly.

EQUIPMENT

Espresso machine	_____
Cart	_____
Grinder(s)	_____
Drip brewer	_____
Awning	_____
Signage (menu, sandwich boards, and so on)	_____
Subtotal:	$_____

LEASEHOLD IMPROVEMENTS

Electrical	_____
Plumbing	_____
Fixtures	_____
Cover, shelter, cabinets/counters	_____
Subtotal:	$_____

PROFESSIONAL SERVICES

Legal	_____
Accounting	_____
Insurance	_____
Leasing agent	_____
Subtotal:	$_____

PERMITS AND LICENSES

Business license	_____

Health permit _____
Building permit _____
Subtotal: $_____

STARTING INVENTORY AND MISCELLANEOUS*

Coffee _____
Milk _____
Paper products _____
Utensils _____
Serveware _____
Other supplies (such as paper towels,
cleaning materials, etc.) _____
Subtotal: $_____

MARKETING AND ADVERTISING

Grand opening _____
Collateral materials (flyers, punch cards,
handbill menus, coupons, etc.) _____
Advertising _____
Subtotal: $_____

INITIAL PERIOD AFTER OPENING

Renewable supplies (milk, coffee,
bakery goods, etc.) _____
Rent _____
Labor _____
Loan interest _____
Personal expenses (what you need to live) _____
Subtotal: $_____

Total Start-Up Costs: $_____

* *Use the "Recommended Beginning Inventory List" on page 113 to help figure these costs.*

want a favorable return on her investment. Either she's given you the money with the understanding that at an established time you'll return the initial capital along with a predetermined "interest" payment, or she's taken a larger risk by banking on the success of your business and negotiating a long-term profit share.

The greater your profitability, the higher her reward. Your business will be most attractive as an investment if the eventual payback on the loan significantly exceeds what your investor can earn through "safer" avenues. In other words, your espresso operation has to look better than a savings account.

If you choose to go with an outside investor, it's best to retain professional legal services to structure the terms of your lending solution. Options include forming a limited partnership, general partnership, or corporation. The best fit will depend on your needs and the goals of your investor.

THIRD-PARTY LEASING AGENTS

A popular and highly visible option is the third-party leasing company. This type of financial institution is willing to use the money it has to help finance your equipment purchases. You'll find these agencies listed under "Leasing Services" in the yellow pages, and your equipment suppliers will probably have one or two they recommend as well.

How does a third-party leasing company work? First, you negotiate a deal with the equipment supplier just as if you're going to purchase the item outright. The actual monetary exchange, however, happens between the supplier and the leasing company. It is the leasing company who is technically buying the cart, espresso machine, or grinder.

You sign a third-party leasing agreement with the leasing company, committing to deliver a monthly payment to them in exchange for the use of "their" equipment. This monthly fee is a sly kind of interest rate—but you'll never hear that term used.

The first and last monthly payments are typically required by the leasing company as an initial deposit on the equipment. After

67

a certain number of payments, when the balance of the piece is paid off, it is the lease company who owns the goods. The most common timeline for this type of leasing agreement is three years, after which time the user can purchase the equipment for a "residual balance." The amount of the residual balance may, or may not, be established up front. (Residuals usually amount to about 10% of the original purchase price.)

Minus a traditional down payment, the up-front cost of financing in this way is low (but don't forget that initial "deposit"). A new business owner is able to retain his own cash for working capital, and the lease payment is usually tax deductible.

The line between leasing and financing is often elusive, but the definition of leasing carries strategic tax implications: lease payments are classified as a business expense rather than a capital investment. In addition, your lease agreement won't show up on your credit report, and therefore won't affect your ability to get a more traditional kind of loan (which you may want down the road for expansion). Financing will. Finally, particularly in a new market where espresso sounds like a very risky venture to mainstream investors, leasing through a company with experience in the industry is a sound financing option. Check into leasing companies and brokers headquartered in regions where espresso is well-established.

As with other types of leasing—cars, for example—third-party agreements can work to your advantage. But don't count on getting a smooth ride. Qualifying for a lease arrangement when you're first getting started isn't easy. Some entrepreneurs try over and over again before they are accepted. And despite its favorable initial outlay, third-party leasing is usually more expensive over time. If you do the calculations carefully, you will usually find that leasing will cost several extra interest points.

The residual balance may sneak up on you as well. Some leasing companies wait until the end of the term to set a residual price. It's their equipment and they can do that. But if you protest too loudly against the final figure, your leasing company will smugly welcome you to look elsewhere.

Don't feel discouraged in the face of these drawbacks. Above all, don't give up. But do evaluate your options strategically. Shop around. In-house leasing through equipment suppliers is becoming more popular, and may offer a promising alternative.

Wherever you find the financial support for your espresso venture, chart your expenses and cover them wisely. Remember that your business, like any other enterprise, will need a little time to get going. Your task as the owner is to do whatever it takes to see your business through to profitability.

Checklist: Financing Your Venture

____ **Determine start-up costs**

    ____ Complete start-up costs worksheet

    ____ Estimate beginning inventory (p.113) to supplement
worksheet

____ **Identify and evaluate financing options**

    ____ Explore personal, institutional, and leasing options

    ____ Calculate total cost of each

    ____ Identify pros and cons of each based on your individual
business goals

____ **Secure financing**

    ____ Determine what the financing agency requires, and prepare
a packet with your business plan and relevant materials
for application

    ____ Contract legal advice, if necessary, to finalize terms

CHAPTER 6
Selecting Your Suppliers

We believe the topic of selecting suppliers is so important it deserves a chapter all of its own.

Your suppliers are your business partners. As with any other business, you need your suppliers to do what they say they're going to do, and when.

Unlike other businesses, however—and like the nature of espresso itself—the effects of a delayed coffee shipment or machine malfun-ction are unusually concentrated. No espresso machine, no sales. And the solution does not rest with you; it's up to your coffee supplier or your machine service person to get things running. Expert, dependable suppliers are more than worth the price of your business. Literally.

A supplier is anyone who supplies anything to you. There are two basic categories: the one-time supplier, like your espresso machine sales person, and the vendor who supplies you in an ongoing way—your coffee roaster, for example. Both are critical. When making contact with potential suppliers, make sure to:

1. Start evaluating the moment a prospective supplier answers the phone. Are they, and their office personnel, helpful? Even if you are simply asking questions? Are they professional? Friendly? Do they take a personal interest in you and your business ideas?

2. Ask how they can contribute to your success beyond providing their primary service or product. What extras do they provide? Will a syrup distributor give you recipes for Italian sodas? Will an espresso machine supplier train you to use the thing? Look for strong after-sales service concerning both operation and maintenance. Find out how well informed they are about industry trends, on a large scale and locally.

3. Insist on a clear demonstration of product features and benefits. Preferably, this takes place in a showroom where you have lots of room for hands-on experimentation and questioning—but a retail setting will do. Make sure the supplier can articulate not only the features of a particular product, but specifically what benefits those features offer you as a user.

4. Seek out suppliers who appreciate the reciprocal nature of your partnership. If you are successful, so will they be. Your suppliers are the allies who will teach you your business by supporting you within the domain of their expertise; they should get to know the needs of your customers and help you to meet them. Your suppliers should be willing to work with you into the future, even if on the surface yours is a one-time sale.

5. Request references, and follow up on them. Although you may begrudge the time up front, it won't be wasted. Visit sites where the supplier has equipment installed or product in use. Speak with customers. Ask, specifically, what kind of ongoing support the supplier has provided. Look for suppliers with both experience and a good reputation.

6. Avoid focusing too heavily on price. Yes, you have a budget to which you must adhere. But remember that you get what you pay for. Don't shop simply for the lowest price; it's usually not the best deal.

7. Take all the time you need to make decisions. Don't let anyone pressure you into a "quick" sale. They can't possibly have your best interests in mind.

The total spectrum of suppliers you need will depend on the range and shape of your espresso business. Of primary concern will be the people who furnish you with espresso equipment (your espresso machine, grinder, and brewer) and renewable products such as coffee, dairy products, and paper goods. Appendix A provides an initial reference list of quality brands, suppliers and resources. The next chapter details what to look for in the equipment you will need to buy, starting with the backbone of your business—the espresso machine.

CHAPTER 7
Buying the
Right Equipment

The Espresso Machine

The espresso machine is the denominator common to every type of espresso operation. There is a big difference in quality among the machines available, and the quality of the machine has a tremendous impact on the quality of the coffee you are able to serve. Understand these differences, and choose wisely.

First, a bit of background. There are approximately 50 separate brands of espresso machines sold in North America, and 80% of them are Italian. It makes sense; Italy is where the espresso tradition developed. There are, however, sizable differences between the espresso consumed here and in Venice.

In the United States, we enjoy our espresso with what the Italians consider to be VAST quantities of milk. While Italians steam milk for less than 20% of all espresso drinks served, we use steamed milk in over 95%. The amount of steam generated to heat and foam milk has a profound effect on a machine's average brewing temperature, which in turn has a tremendous effect on espresso quality. When brewing temperature becomes unstable (which is what happens when excessive steaming taxes the machine), coffee quality suffers.

In addition, the parts of the espresso machine that are impacted by steaming must be more durable in the U.S. Our penchant for milk affects steam wands, boiler pressure gauges, and steam valves. Steam valves on our machines, in fact, require four to five times the maintenance their Italian counterparts do.

Test a dealer's knowledge by inquiring about his opinions on these issues. Ask potential machine suppliers what parts availability and service expertise they can offer in light of this trend. What provisions for repair do they make?

In the United States, espresso is associated with "gourmet" coffee. In Italy, espresso is coffee. It's not considered an especially gourmet product. Like many aspects of the Italian lifestyle, their espresso has more flair and is of a higher quality than everyday coffee elsewhere. Bear in mind, however, that about 40% of the beans used by most Italian roasters are robusta—a low-grown, disease-resistant, harsh-tasting species of coffee bean that is higher in caffeine and lower in cost than what we consider specialty coffee. Add to that the fact that very few espresso bar owners buy their own espresso machines. Usually, the roasters do that for them, and their emphasis is on keeping costs down.

The point is not by any means to knock Italian coffee or equipment, but to shed a bit of light on the espresso machine market. Just because it's Italian doesn't mean it's necessarily top quality. In the United States, the profit to be made on espresso is a result of its appeal as a high-quality, specialty product. To realize that profit, you've got to make it well. Exquisitely well. Quality is what will make or break you, and the machine you choose has a lot to do with the final quality of your cup.

Espresso Machine Size

Espresso machines are rated primarily by size and category of operation. Size is expressed by number of "groups," the group being the actual port where a shot of espresso is brewed. Espresso machines range in size from one to four groups. The number of groups on a given machine indicates the boiler size of the machine: a one-group machine typically has a boiler which ranges in volume from 4–6 liters; a two-group measures 8–12 liters; a three-group, 15–18 liters; and a four-group, 21–25 liters.

Each group can brew one or two shots at a time; some operators will pull triples on a group, but this approach requires

Diagram of a Typical Espresso Machine

The two-group volumetric automatic espresso machine is the most popular among commercial users.

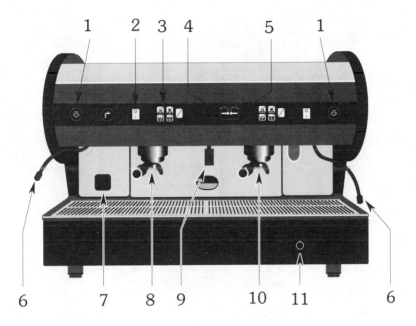

1. Steam valve

2. Manual brew switch
   (overrides automatic)

3. Brew button pad

4. Pump pressure gauge

5. Boiler pressure gauge

6. Steam wand

7. On/off switch

8. Double portafilter

9. Hot water nozzle

10. Single portafilter

11. Manual boiler
    fill valve

Illustration courtesy of Espresso Specialists, Inc.

Espresso Machine Group Components

The size of an espresso machine is described by its number of "groups," the group being the actual port where a shot of espresso is brewed. To brew espresso, the barista fits a portafilter full of ground, compacted coffee into the group casting. Hot water is then dispensed from the group and down through the coffee, pouring into the awaiting shot glasses or brew pitchers.

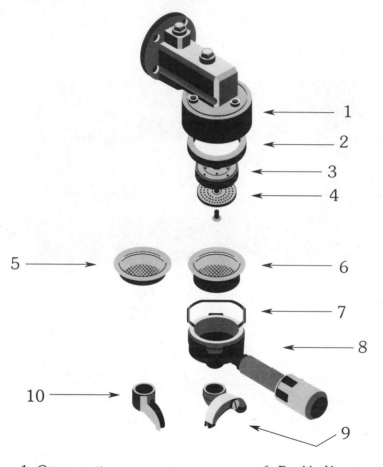

1. Group casting

2. Group portafilter gasket

3. Diffusion block

4. Dispersion screen

5. Single filter insert

6. Double filter insert

7. Insert retaining spring

8. Portafilter

9. Double spout

10. Single spout

 Illustration courtesy of Espresso Specialists, Inc.

extraordinarily high volume to be practical. Theoretically, each group is capable of pouring two shots every 30 seconds. A bit of math will tell you that's 240 shots of espresso every hour. Sounds like big bucks, eh? Here's the hitch: there are too many other factors involved in preparing espresso beverages, not the least of which is the human factor, to make good on that statistic.

Any sales person who quotes his machine's "capacity" is no doubt giving you a true figure, but that figure can not necessarily be replicated in a working environment. Remember the challenge of balancing steam power and brewing temperature?

Functionality is not simply a product of the number of groups available, but a result of a complicated combination of interrelated factors. Spend time with people who use the machines you're considering to get the real story on performance.

CATEGORIES OF OPERATION:
AUTOMATIC, SEMI-AUTOMATIC, AND MANUAL

The precise naming of each category of operation is a function of time and automation. The most recent level of automation is usually referred to as an "automatic," while its predecessors are termed semi-automatic and manual. A more profound discussion of levels of automation will help you tell them apart no matter what they might be called in the showroom.

Manual machines are the old lever operated style, technically archaic but offering the aesthetic experience of literally "pulling shots." The manual machine uses a piston and heavy-duty spring to produce brewing pressure. This machinery is deeply traditional and, as such, is valued by some baristas. A manual machine is the only option for the operator who is restricted to propane for his energy source; it can be configured to require no electricity beyond heat for operation.

A semi-automatic espresso machine uses a pump and motor combination to drive water through the coffee grounds. Pushing a switch or lever generally activates the brewing process. The machine pump continues to run water through the grounds until its operator has deactivated that switch. Advantages over the manual machine are a more consistent brewing pressure, and no moving parts that require extra care. Regardless of brand, semi-automatic machines tend to be very reliable. They also require great expertise and vigilance from the barista during brewing.

Automatic, or volumetric automatic, espresso machines also use a pump and motor. Their technology also includes a solid state microprocessing system that measures water for each and every cup. This sophisticated system determines when to shut off water flow during brewing. Because the easiest and most common way to ruin a shot of espresso is to let too much water run through the grounds, thereby overextracting the coffee, the water-monitoring feature greatly reduces the risk of bad brewing. This machine has become first choice for many top restaurants and large-scale espresso bars.

As you might expect, however, the electronic portion of the machine tends to be the most problem-prone, and the most difficult for a lay person to diagnose and repair. If you are in a remote location or are not confident in your supplier's ability to respond quickly, give careful consideration to using a semi-automatic machine and well-marked shot glasses and measuring the flow yourself. This is a perfectly acceptable and effective approach; it just requires a little more personnel training up front.

There is, technically, one additional machine category: fully automatic. This type of machine grinds, packs, and brews the coffee—no hands! Some models even steam milk and measure it into your cup. Fully automatic machines are the fastest-growing segment of the espresso machine industry. They require more specialized repair and servicing, but less training and operational expertise, than other espresso machines. The machines are entirely appropriate for institutional or self-service environments, but can't provide that touch of soul that draws customers back again and again. They produce the same drink repetitively, without room for small variations or personal panache.

The two-group automatic espresso machine is the most popular among commercial users, and can cost anywhere from

$3,500 to just under $10,000. This is an excellent choice if you are a startup deli and want to offer espresso as a sideline; by the time the equipment no longer meets your needs, you're in a good place to upgrade. For any business that plans a greater focus on espresso, fewer than two groups will prove woefully inadequate.

Regardless of which type of machine you eventually choose, it should in all cases feature automatic water fill. This prevents the unit from running dry and burning up heating elements.

POD TECHNOLOGY

In addition to the various levels of automation, there is a relatively new permutation on the market: pod technology. Pods are preground, premeasured, and individually packaged doses of espresso. Some can be brewed on regular machines and some require special adaptive technology, while others necessitate a completely different machine.

Chapter 8, Choosing Your Coffee, describes the pros and cons of using pod espresso. The pod sector, though young, is a rapidly evolving one; we'll no doubt hear more about pod technology in the near future.

IDENTIFYING A MACHINE'S ABILITY TO BREW GOOD ESPRESSO

First and foremost, you want to buy a machine that can brew a good shot of espresso. Most are capable of doing so, but always insist on proof. Don't settle for word-of-mouth. Don't commit to buy a machine until, with your own eyes, you have seen it pull a great shot.

How will you know that great shot when you see it? Make a close visual inspection. Good espresso has a thick, rich, golden brown crema. This feature is indispensable. The crema is the sweet part of the coffee, where the sugars are contained. The crema should cling lazily to the sides of the shot glass or miniature pitcher into which it was brewed, and should last for a full minute before beginning to break apart.

Taste it. The taste of good espresso is strong, potent, and may shock you with its zing. Contrary to popular perception, it is NOT bitter. Nor does good espresso taste burnt. Instead, the flavors of a good espresso may range from butter to caramel to spice. After its initial bite, espresso should be smooth.

Poor espresso is not necessarily the fault of the machine. There are so many variables at play. Familiarize yourself with these (you may find Chapter 12, Ensuring Espresso Drink Quality, helpful), and watch the brewing process carefully. Take note of the freshness of the coffee, the quality of the water, the precision of the barista. Analyze the elements, weighing individual performance over the sum total of the espresso in your cup. If the espresso doesn't measure up, politely challenge the sales person to brew you a better one.

TROUBLESHOOTING MAINTENANCE AND REPAIR

Set yourself up to avoid down-time. Whether the supplier does repairs himself or refers business to a service technician, make sure your espresso machine is going to get the service it needs.

Does the service provider keep a full supply of parts on hand? Don't just take his word for it—make him show you a workbench or parts board bursting with equipment. Ask him how he will follow through on service commitments, both prescheduled and emergency. Ask about the preventive maintenance schedule he recommends. See Chapter 14, Equipment Maintenance, to get a feel for what kind of response you should hear.

ADDITIONAL FEATURES TO LOOK FOR

• *Features that help protect you against down-time.* A good example is "semi-automatic override," which allows the barista to operate an automatic machine manually if an electronic malfunction should occur.

• *A capable boiler system and good "recovery time."* This is indicated by the ability to handle multiple steaming and brewing tasks without a sacrifice of either brew quality or power. You can test recovery time by ordering five two-shot, twelve-ounce lattes in a row. A machine with good recovery time should not flinch. (A visible flinch would be the noticeable decrease in steaming power.) Ask your sales person for this demonstration, or order the drinks from an espresso stand using one of his machines. And don't forget to write the cost off as a business expense.

Certain manufacturers have increased the size of their boilers to accommodate the higher demands of the U.S. marketplace. The Italian company La Marzocco invented and has been the leading manufacturer of a two-boiler system, which is more effective than any other design in maintaining both consistency of brewing temperature and overall steaming power.

• *Increased "cup height" under the groups.* This is a convenience feature designed for the American market. Thermal sixteen-ounce cups were an innovation here, and are too tall to fit under most groups. Originally, espresso machines were designed to accommodate the diminutive Italian demitasse cup.

Why would you want to squeeze that monster cup under a group? Because brewing directly into the serving cup helps to preserve espresso quality. Look for about eight inches.

• *Ergonomic design.* Comfort and ease of use can play an important role in quality brewing during times of high volume. Like the curve of a car seat or a particular kind of underwear, the best functional design is a matter of personal preference. Try out any machine—ideally, a wide variety of them—before making your purchase.

Appendix A contains a list of good, safe espresso machine bets—all well-established market leaders. There are others we'd recommend, and some new ones on the horizon. Combine common sense with the information and advice you get from potential suppliers. Avoid being under- or oversold. Figure out what you need a machine to do in order to meet your business goals, and use that information to make a sound buying decision.

The Grinder

Great espresso is made from freshly ground coffee beans. There's simply no way around it; you're going to need a dedicated espresso grinder. If you encounter an espresso machine supplier who insinuates that good coffee can be produced without an on-site grinder, take this as an indication of the extent of her knowledge. Beware.

There are two possible exceptions: when you're trying to offer decaf in severely limited space, and if you decide to brew espresso pods instead of ground espresso.

If you just can't fit a second grinder on your cart, you can get away with pregrinding one day's worth of decaffeinated espresso beans. Store this coffee in an airtight container, spooning it out for use upon demand. As the cart owner, you'll have to determine your own freshness standards and keep tabs on the volume of decaf served; when you have the space and budget to add a decaf grinder, do so.

The espresso grinder itself has two purposes. The first is to grind coffee beans evenly into a fine powder. Most models utilize flat burrs to do this; one spins while the other remains stationary, and centrifugal force sends the coffee beans through. The distance between these burrs is what determines the fineness of the coffee grounds as they emerge. Some ultra high-end models use a conical burr, which grinds at a slower speed but communicates less undesirable heat to the beans. (These are not readily available in the United States.)

The second purpose of the grinder is to "dose," or measure, the powdery coffee grounds into even portions. Accurate portioning ensures that the barista achieves the correct ratio of coffee to water during brewing. Although grinders are categorized by size, grinder capacity is usually not an issue. Grinder volume, the power of the motor coupled with the size of the grinding burrs inside, is. It's important to watch a grinder in operation to see how its motor keeps pace with demand.

In addition, you want a machine that can be adjusted—for fineness and coarseness of grind—with ease and efficiency.

Diagram of a Typical Espresso Grinder-Doser

A grinder has two purposes: to grind coffee beans into a fine, even powder; and to "dose," or measure, these grounds into consistent portions.

1. Bean hopper
2. Adjusting collar
3. Grinding burr mounting collar
4. Top grinding burr
5. Bottom grinding burr
6. Timer
7. Doser

Illustration courtesy of Espresso Specialists, Inc.

Although some folks out there will tell you it's true, there is no such thing as a self-adjusting grinder. Nor does any particular "click stop" on the grinder's outer gear indicate the perfect grind. The process of adjusting grind is both reactive—to fluctuations in temperature and humidity, for example—and ongoing. Note: doser-grinders should not be used for other types of coffee grinding. The machinery is too carefully calibrated for the fine grind required by the espresso brewing process to be practical for drip coffee or bulk sales.

The final difference between doser-grinders is their level of automation. The more automation they have, the more they cost and the less energy you have to invest in keeping the dosing chamber full of grounds. The most basic models come with a manual switch: "on" sets the grinder in motion, "off" shuts it off. The next level sports a timer which can be activated at will to trigger a set period of grinding. Finally, there are "super automatic" grinders which keep their own dosing chambers full with a weight-sensitive mechanism.

Look for a model that allows for easy removal of its chamber lid, so you can quickly reintroduce ground coffee to the chamber if you overdose. Don't pay any attention to built-in tampers, which are usually mounted on the outside of the dosing chamber. Proper tamping technique does not include using one.

A good barista maintains a consistent balance between tamping and adjusting grind to pull a good shot. Powerful compacting of the coffee grounds in the portafilter, or tamping, is necessary to introduce enough resistance to the pressure of the brewing water to yield the correct rate of pour. A proper tamp leverages about 50 pounds per square inch. Here's the rub: the average weight of a grinder is 30 pounds. Using a mounted tamper, it is physically impossible to achieve an adequate tamp without lifting the machine off the counter. If you buy a grinder that sports a built-in tamper, we recommend removing it and furnishing employees with a hand-held model.

Make your choice based on the projected volume of your espresso operation, overall equipment and supplier quality, and the depth of your pockets. A budget of between $600 and $800 will buy just about anyone whatever they need. Appendix A contains a list of reliable grinder brands; there are other quality options, but this is a good place to start.

The Drip Brewer

Although drip-brewed coffee is not a direct part of the espresso operation, it is often a peripheral or complementary one. We'll discuss considerations briefly here and, should you decide to include drip-brewed in your coffee program, encourage you to seek further brewing and equipment guidelines from your coffee roaster. If you are bringing espresso into a restaurant or retail environment where drip coffee already has a presence, work carefully with your coffee supplier to make sure the quality, taste, and presentation of espresso and drip coffee complement each other well. Your supplier can also help you navigate drip coffee grinding options.

Start evaluating options by brewing temperature; the best drip coffee is brewed at around 197°F. To eliminate waste and keep coffee as fresh as possible for customers, a machine that brews directly into an airpot is recommended. Make sure the machine you choose will brew the proper ratio of coffee (two tablespoons per six-ounce cup) without overflowing.

The easiest place to get a good machine is probably going to be from your coffee supplier. Most suppliers furnish brewers to augment their businesses, because so many coffee customers are offices, hotels, restaurants, and so on. Other machine sources include restaurant supply houses and cash-and-carry type outlets. The price for a drip brewer with airpot ranges from $100 to $1,000, and includes a range of sizes, materials, and functions.

Remember that for drip-loving customers, there is a viable espresso option: the Americano. An Americano is a drip-strength cup of coffee made right on the espresso machine with a combination of fresh-brewed espresso and hot water. Trying an

Americano may be a stretch for some, so as an operator you may want to offer incentive—like a freebie—if you want to promote it. Many customers find they ardently prefer its taste.

Water Treatment

Ninety-nine percent of a cup of coffee is water. There is no coffee that tastes better than the quality of the water that brews it. And the taste quality of plumbed water, especially these days, is becoming increasingly questionable. What can you do?

WATER FILTRATION

For the water that runs into your espresso machine, a good filtration system is wholeheartedly recommended. A typical system uses a combination paper and carbon filter to remove foul taste, odor, and any stuff you might chew (particulate matter). Filtering alone is a great way to make coffee better.

Filtration systems range in size from smaller models, installed just prior to the espresso machine, to systems large enough to take care of an entire building. At the very least, your espresso machine should have its own $20–$100 water filter, good for about three months, to screen out the inevitable guck. This filter is a cheap insurance policy for a very expensive machine.

WATER SOFTENING

Water softening is not as easy. Fortunately, it's not always necessary. "Hard" water is high in mineral content, and it causes a terrible buildup called scale. Softening will remove excess mineral content from the water. You can find out if you're in an area with hard water by looking for deposits—usually calcium, lime, and magnesium—on your household hot water heater or ice maker. A quick call to your city water department will also answer the question.

These mineral deposits wreak havoc on an espresso machine. Operating with hard water, a machine can clog up in just one month. When it clogs, it simply ceases to operate, necessitating expensive repair and costly down-time.

The degree of hardness in your water should be matched equally by efforts to remedy it. For low to medium hardness, use disposable water-softening cartridges. If the water in your area is of a medium to high level of hardness, you'll probably need a more elaborate reverse osmosis system. There is also a type of small, rechargeable water softener typically available from espresso machine suppliers. This kind of softener works quite well if the operator is dedicated to recharging it (about once every two weeks is recommended).

Contact a local water specialist to find out what's necessary; try the yellow pages under water treatment or filtration. Appendix A lists the names of some expert sources and brands to get you started. Many espresso machine dealers are also mini-experts on area water as well because they deal with its effects so regularly.

Espresso Carts

If you need to purchase an espresso cart or kiosk configuration, apply the same high standards we encourage you to use when purchasing your espresso machine.

Be able to articulate exactly what will be demanded of the structure. What features does your health department require? What physical dimensions will be appropriate? Countless are the times that a novice espresso entrepreneur has ordered a slick, shiny, and costly new cart only to discover, upon delivery, that the cart won't fit through the door of its intended operating space. Don't let this happen to you. Think through all of the physical and material considerations carefully.

Seek out the same follow-up service you want from your machine distributor. Carts, with fewer automatic components and electrical functions, are less prone to mechanical problems. But the smooth functioning of your cart is equally crucial to the profitability of your business. In addition, cart suppliers are often savvy resources concerning health department requirements, at the very least in their own region and often beyond.

The typical cart is essentially a box on wheels. The construction of this box should include a countertop and working surface, space to create attractive displays (usually folding wings of some kind that spread once the cart is in its operating location), and room for pastries and other sale items.

Many manufacturers are now building modular units, or side carts, to facilitate high-volume drip brewing. In some areas, constructing entire kiosks—one central cart combined with several adjoining modular units—is becoming more and more common. These new add-ons facilitate storage and increase the opportunities to sell extra food products, broaden drip coffee offerings, and add other major food categories like granita.

In some areas, however, the health department prohibits the use of these extra units. Check with your health department before investing in modular additions. Virtually every health department requires the cart to sport a hand sink with both hot and cold running water, an appropriate fresh water supply, and a drain waste facility. Most carts have to have under-the-counter refrigerator units with NSF approval.

An individual with good cabinetry skills might want to try and build her own espresso cart. If you are an adventuresome carpenter type, remember that the espresso machine requires certain specialized functions you'll need to add. High-pressure water delivered to the machine, appropriate voltage, and the right kind of water system are among these.

Ask a few suppliers; they'll offer valuable advice about how to pull it off. There are also several companies that sell cart components for the moderate do-it-yourselfer. Appendix A contains a beginning list of cart and kiosk suppliers and kit-makers to help you get started.

Potential Equipment Suppliers: Questions to Ask

Get the most value for your time! Formulating a list of questions for vendors—and using it during your initial meetings with them— ensures thoroughness and consistency. Here is a list of the inquiries you may have for potential equipment suppliers.

1. Which brands and models do you sell?

2. What are the features and benefits of each product?
   A feature is useless if it doesn't benefit the user. Feature: stainless steel steam wands on an espresso machine. Benefits: these steam wands are long-lasting (and therefore less expensive in the long run), easily replaceable, and easily cleaned.

3. What is included in the warranty?

4. What kind of operational training do you provide?

5. What industry insights (for example, popular menu items) can you provide that will help make my espresso business successful?

6. How can you help with financing?

7. How many pieces of equipment have you sold for use in a setting similar to mine? Why is your equipment a good match for my goals?

8. What can you tell me about industry trends in this area?

9. Do you have a customer list? Whom would you suggest I contact for a referral? Who else?

10. What is your response time in the event of an emergency? Would this response time be guaranteed in our contract?

11. Is in-house service available, or do I call someone else? What are the qualifications of your service people?

12. Can you provide me with resources to obtain other items (cups, utensils, etc.) necessary for my business?

13. What regulatory and safety approvals (UL, NSF, etc.) does your equipment carry?

Checklist: Buying Equipment

___ **Purchase a high-quality espresso machine**

   ___ Use supplier questionnaire to gather information about different espresso machines and sources, including:
      ___ Features and benefits of different brands and models
      ___ Warranties and safety approvals
      ___ Training for your personnel
      ___ Additional support and access to industry resources
      ___ Service and repair
      ___ Financing
   ___ Make sure you taste a good shot off the machine
   ___ *Check references*

___ **Buy a good grinder(s)**

   ___ Gather information about the features and benefits of different brands, models and sources, paying particular attention to:
      ___ Grinder volume
      ___ Ease and efficiency of grind adjustment
      ___ Level of automation (what's best for your business?)

___ **If you decide to offer drip coffee, purchase your brewer**

   ___ Consult your coffee roaster for brewing and equipment guidelines, remembering to screen for temperature (197°F)
   ___ Take space and logistical requirements into account

___ **Investigate and implement proper water treatment**

   ___ Choose and install a water filtration system
   ___ Determine the "hardness" of your water supply, and work with a local water treatment expert to soften if necessary

___ **If applicable, find a well-designed espresso cart**

   ___ Investigate health department requirements, and make sure any cart you consider meets each of them!
   ___ Evaluate based on component quality and design features
   ___ Screen suppliers for follow-up service and repair
   ___ *Check references*

CHAPTER 8
Choosing
Your Coffee

Beyond choosing vendors for your coffee-preparing equipment, the next most important partner to find is your coffee supplier. Your relationship with the coffee supplier is an important, multifaceted one. In many ways, your operation will be an extension of their business—you will be representing their brand, and the quality of the coffee you serve will reflect positively or negatively on them. By the same token, it is in the coffee supplier's best interests to make sure you have all the tools you need to serve the highest quality cup.

Espresso

To launch a successful espresso operation, you will need high quality, fresh-roasted coffee. There's absolutely no substitute for it. Check out your local roasters; there are new microroasters springing up everywhere, and they offer some tremendous coffees. You'll need both regular and decaffeinated. Because coffee will be the focus of your espresso operation, and great coffee your biggest selling point, choose wisely.

ARABICA VS. ROBUSTA

There are two species of commercial coffee bean: *robusta* and *arabica*. Robusta beans grow at low altitudes, are disease-resistant and economical, and taste decidedly inferior in the cup. Many Italian espresso blends feature robustas, primarily because green coffee is extremely expensive in Italy. While the Italians are masters at incorporating these beans to maximum effect, and Italian-style espresso blends have become increasingly available to consumers worldwide, we recommend that the coffee you serve be 100% arabica. Arabica beans are simply a finer species of bean. Arabicas are grown at dramatically higher altitudes and feature more desirable and pleasurable flavor characteristics.

TASTE

Most roasters feature their own custom espresso blend, a combination of coffees formulated to perform well on an espresso machine. A good espresso is complex, well-balanced, and typically roasted slightly darker than coffees designed for drip brewing. That said, there is a huge range of acceptable tastes, blends, roasts, etc., that constitutes good espresso.

Taste the options. But don't necessarily base a final decision on your own preference—yours might not reflect your audience's. Do some detective work to find out what goes over well in your market. What are other coffee places serving? Does the local newspaper sponsor an annual "Best Of…" competition? Is there a category for coffee? Who won? The supplier should be able to offer useful insights. Poll a variety of roasters.

Whether you want to go with an espresso blend, other recommended coffee, or a custom blend your supplier develops especially for you, expect service. Look for someone who is willing to work with you. Period.

PRICE

A dollar per pound difference translates to only about $.02 per cup, so excellent coffee is absolutely worth the expense. An outstanding cup will draw a crowd of regulars. Depending on your type of operation, many of them may visit you several times each week—if not every day—and it is their repeat business that will make you successful.

FRESHNESS AND FREQUENCY OF SUPPLY

Because coffee is a vulnerable and perishable food product, find a supplier who makes frequent deliveries or uses a coffee packaging technology that guarantees good shelf life. (Once exposed to air, coffee beans maintain their freshness for about one week.)

Look for the vacuum-sealed bags with one-way valves used by many roasters, which should be conspicuously marked with roast date or "death" date (the day on which the coffee should be retired if still unused). These bags can be stored for a finite amount of time, sometimes up to 90 days, before being opened for use. Because your ability to store large shipments may be limited, aim for smaller deliveries, more often.

There is a fairly new espresso packaging technology that seals espresso coffee into individual "pods." (See Chapter 7, Buying the Right Equipment, for a discussion of the machines used to brew them.) Pods rule out a number of the variables involved in brewing espresso, thereby contributing to overall consistency in the cup. Volume of dose, regularity of grind, concentration of tamp—each of these aspects of espresso brewing requires a great deal of experience and expertise, and pods reduce each of these things to a constant.

For large food services hesitant about being able to guarantee consistency from operator to operator, pods may be a welcome solution. And there's cleanliness to consider: self-contained pods are substantially tidier than regular ground espresso.

One hitch with using pods is the issue of freshness; the different types of packaging materials used vary in effectiveness. Some roasters package pods individually, while others produce vacuum bags with a 24- or 36-hour supply. Another drawback is the expense. The price of both pods and the special equipment required to brew them is high, the pods alone going for approximately two to three times the unit cost of ground coffee. Pods do, however, eliminate the need for—and initial investment of—buying a grinder.

Drip Coffee

The specialty nature of your espresso menu will make customer expectations of your entire coffee program higher. Don't sabotage overall potential by serving an inferior drip coffee. In newer markets, remember that good drip coffee can also be used to pull people in to try the higher-margin espresso drinks.

Espresso operators with limited storage space may want to find a coffee that can be used with equal success on both the espresso and drip machines. These blends certainly exist, often combining bright Latin American varietals with earthier, full-bodied Indonesian coffees and a distinct measure of dark roast. Despite the fact that you may use the same coffee on both machines, however, listen to your supplier when she says that very different grinds are needed for each brewing method! Once ground, the coffees will have to be kept separate; interchangeability will only take you so far in the fight for extra space.

That said, some operators who are squeezed for space decide not to offer drip-brewed coffee at all. Some offer regular, but not decaffeinated; the volume for the latter is usually so much less. A good espresso alternative for drip coffee lovers, and a decaf option that doesn't require extra brewing space, is the Americano. Again, an Americano is a drip-strength combination of espresso and hot water.

If you are in a restaurant situation, there's a good chance you already serve drip coffee. Espresso was never meant to replace drip coffee, nor will its addition curtail your orders for it. As you enhance your coffee program with espresso, however, consider switching to the french press for your drip coffee brewing method. Remember that specialty coffee can be a very high profit add-on product, and upgrading drip coffee options will contribute favorably to both your image and your margin.

The french press, a simple glass apparatus with a wire mesh plunger, offers coffee drinkers the most direct and flavorful drip-type coffee experience. It most closely resembles the brewing method used by coffee tasters in their "cupping" rooms. The french press mixes coarsely ground coffee and just-off-boil water for four minutes, after which time the wire mesh filter is plunged down through the brew and traps the grounds at the bottom of the pot. Coffee in a french press retains most of its heat and all of its desirable flavor characteristics for about twenty minutes. This is a perfectly elegant way to bring coffee to a dining table.

If you do well, so will your supplier. Your roaster will appreciate the way you're representing his coffee, and will appreciate you as a customer. Again, this relationship should be a mutually interested one, with each party contributing to the success of the other party's business. When you find a good coffee relationship, we recommend sticking with it, through thick and thin, yours and theirs. It's good for everyone's business.

Potential Coffee Suppliers: Questions to Ask

Here is a list of questions you may want to ask potential coffee suppliers. Keep it handy, and add your own queries to it as your research progresses.

1. What coffees do you have that are specifically roasted and blended for espresso brewing? How many are there? What decaffeinated options do you have?

2. How is your coffee packaged? What is your recommended shelf life for coffee stored in an unopened container? Once the container has been opened?

3. How many days per week do you roast?

4. What are the order and delivery days for my area?

5. What is your minimum order?

6. What kind of espresso-brewing training and expertise can you offer me and my employees?

7. Can you provide me with the names of some businesses that serve your espresso, so I can sample the coffee there?

8. Do you have drip-brewing equipment for loan or lease?

9. Do you supply other items, such as flavoring syrups, that will complement my operation?

Checklist: Choosing Your Coffee

____ **Identify potential suppliers, including:**

    ____ Local roasters

    ____ Long-distance/large-scale wholesalers

____ **Gather coffee samples for each category of coffee you're considering serving**

    ____ Espresso

    ____ Decaffeinated espresso

    ____ Drip coffee

    ____ Decaffeinated drip coffee

    ____ Coffee(s) that might be used for both espresso and drip brewing

____ **Taste, taste, taste**

    ____ Attend tastings with coffee wholesale representatives

    ____ Solicit friends' and associates' opinions

    ____ Keep tasting to develop your own palate

____ **Use the supplier questionnaire to gather additional information about sources, including:**

    ____ Freshness standards and packaging

    ____ Service and delivery

    ____ Training

    ____ Pricing and minimum orders

    ____ Availability of brewing equipment

CHAPTER 9
Accessories and Renewable Supplies

Imagine yourself standing behind the counter, going through the motions of making a mocha or other espresso drink. What items do you use in the process? Mocha pump. Milk, a steaming pitcher, and shot glasses. Timer? The knock box. A paper to-go cup, complete with dome lid.

To create your own accessory list, read through the descriptions that follow, as well as the recommended opening inventory summary on page 113. Skim through industry magazines and espresso supply catalogs (see Appendix A). Study Chapter 12, Ensuring Espresso Drink Quality, and the glossary at the end of the book to gain an understanding of how these accessories are used. Watch a few seasoned operators to decide which collateral tools will help you make the best drinks, in the shortest amount of time, and with the greatest measure of ease.

Accessorizing Your Espresso Operation

Where both physical size and overall expense are concerned, accessories—or "hard supplies"—comprise a category that falls somewhere between large equipment and renewable supplies. Espresso accessories can be obtained through a variety of sources, including mail-order espresso suppliers, restaurant supply houses, or your local cash-and-carry. Buy wisely! The detailed descriptions and purchasing hints on the pages that follow should aid you in doing so.

Steaming pitcher. Every espresso machine operator needs commercial-grade steaming pitchers to steam the milk for espresso drinks. Sizes range from 12 to 60 ounces. You'll get the best start with a one-liter or 32-ounce model. Because the volume of each pitcher full will double during steaming, a 32-ounce pitcher is optimal to hold enough milk and foam for two or three drinks. A good steaming pitcher will last many years.

Look for high-grade stainless steel with a solid, welded-on handle. Steel wears well and lets the operator monitor the milk heat accurately by touch. A rolled pouring edge works best, especially as you become more adept and can control the mix of foam and milk in your drinks during the pour. In most North American markets, a wide array of milks is served; it's best to have pitchers accurately marked, with at least one pitcher per fat content type.

Thermometers. Lots of people use thermometers to monitor proper milk temperature. It's very possible to achieve a desirable effect without this technology, but it takes practice. Use of a milk thermometer will ensure consistency and quality, especially among newcomers to the art.

Good milk-steaming thermometers come with a clip for attachment to the side of the pitcher. A thermometer should fit pitchers well, have a large and visible dial, but not get in the way. The most popular and practical range is 0°–220°F.

Spoon/spatula. A good barista doesn't use one of these to spoon foam onto a latte, but to hold it back while pouring—and then *allow* the foam into the drink as appropriate. The most common utensils are the large stainless serving spoons (quite long-handled) and plastic or rubber baker's spatulas.

Hand tamper. The tamper is a small tool shaped somewhat like a mushroom that is used for packing espresso grounds into the portafilter to prepare them for brewing. A proper tamp is applied from above, leveraging weight equal to about 50 pounds per square inch; we will discuss this in greater depth later.

Some doser-grinders are fitted with upside-down tamps. These call for *upward* force from the barista. Such tamps are a remarkably bad invention with no hope of generating the appropriate tamping force, and we recommend taking them off right away. When you purchase your espresso machine, the manufacturer will probably equip you with a tamper or two; these are also typically of variable quality.

Plastic tampers tend to chip and break if dropped. It is better to purchase your own substantial, easy-to-hold anodized aluminum or ultra-hard wood version. There is, again, heated controversy over the nuances: flat surface or convex? Persuasive arguments exist on both sides. Take your pick.

Shot glasses/brew pitchers. There is great debate over the relative merits of clear glass shot glasses versus stainless steel brew pitchers (also called "bell creamers").

Shot glasses hold heat well. Using shot glasses allows you to monitor the quality of drinks visually, which should be done every hour or so whether you're brewing in glasses or not. Look for the variety with a visible one-ounce mark. They do break, so if this is your choice, keep plenty handy. Brew pitchers do not break, which is their primary advantage. Some also have little curved handles, which protect the operator from heat.

It's best to use neither, and brew directly into the cup whenever possible. This method makes sure the sweet crema gets into the drink, instead of being left behind clinging to the sides of the shot glass from which it was poured. During periods of high volume, it saves valuable time for the operator as well.

Shot timers. The purpose of shot timers is to time the extraction of the pour, or pull, of each espresso shot. Some operators live and die by the timing of their shots, which may be taking things a bit too far. Periodic use of a shot timer, however, is a good way to monitor extraction time and make sure the grind is appropriate for optimal extraction.

Don't buy shot timers that count down. Your shot timers need to count up, starting when water first hits the grounds and ending when the pour of a full shot is complete. Some timers can be set for either mode which, if you serve drip coffee and want to keep tabs on its age in the pot, is useful. Timers backed with magnets are handy for sticking to the side of your machines.

Knockbox. This is the box into which the barista knocks spent grounds out of the portafilter after brewing. It's a stainless steel box with a rubber-covered bar across the middle, and either sits on top of the counter by the espresso machine, is recessed, or "bottomless" with a lined wastebasket underneath (this variation is particularly good for high-volume bars). Good knockboxes use the same reinforced rubber found in the auto industry to cover the knocking bar; cheap hose gives long before the box's life should end.

Condiment shakers. Condiments are standard at all bars. The most common are powdered cocoa and vanilla, cinnamon, and nutmeg. Be careful that your condiment dispensers aren't too large; customers will gobble up your condiments inadvertently. If dispensing holes are too small, they'll clog—  frustrating for both you and your customers. The moral is that not just any condiment shaker will do; consider the practicalities with care.

Whipped cream dispensers. A high-quality whipped cream dispenser is much better than buying disposable cans of whipped cream; a good dispenser yields superior whipped cream, won't end up in a landfill, and is ultimately less expensive because it will last for years. Look for a commercial-grade dispenser. Most use nitrous oxide chargers and fresh cream, one pint at a time, that you can get from your dairy supplier.

Mocha pump. Mocha pumps are expensive and can certainly be done without. They are, however, easy and clean to use. They also prevent the necessity of having a name brand squeeze bottle of chocolate syrup out on the counter, which detracts from the mystery and prestige of your gourmet product. Especially if you decide to make your own mocha syrup from cocoa powder, a sturdy stainless steel syrup pump will streamline bar operations.

Pour spouts for syrups. Start with a generous number, twenty-five or so. These help control sticky syrups and cut down the degree to which undesirable insects are attracted to them.

Cleaning brushes. Coffee is so extremely perishable that any left lodged in your machinery will soon spoil the taste of later servings. Nor is it permissible—if you want to ensure freshness—to introduce water to any surface with which your coffee might come in contact before brewing. Brushes are the best way to keep machinery free of errant beans and grounds.

We recommend a modest set: a group cleaning brush with its bristles angled properly for inside the group area of the espresso machine; a paint brush-type grinder brush for the doser (don't skimp here—acids are hard on the nylon of a cheap brush); and a counter brush to keep preparation and service surfaces relatively ground-free. This last item is especially useful if you sell and grind coffee by the pound.

Serving cups. If you're planning on having a cafe or retail store with significant for-here business, it's good to stock a selection of ceramic or glass cups. Available types include everything from cafeteria-style mugs to hand-painted Italian cappuccino cups.

We recommend using commercial-grade serving cups. (But do make sure they look nice.) Be sure to include demitasse cups, as small as possible and with matching spoons and saucers. The best way to serve straight shots of espresso is in a demitasse. Don't spend lots of money on fancy ones, though, because the most attractive varieties have a tendency to slide out the door.

Standard cappuccino cups should hold six to eight ounces of liquid and have wide mouths. Latte cups or mugs tend to hold eight, ten, or even twelve or more ounces of milk. The North American versions of this serveware are still only an approximation of what's available in Europe. When you go to check out a restaurant or bar supply house, be prepared to choose from their selection.

Perishables and Renewable Supplies

When choosing those vendors who will be supplying you with items on a regular basis, it's a good idea to keep the numbers down. Look for suppliers who carry a number of useful items in their inventory. Frequent delivery will help keep your storage needs moderate.

DAIRY PRODUCTS

If you don't already have a good milk source for your current business, there are several good options available to you. You can deal directly with a dairy, establish a relationship with an independent milk delivery driver, or make your own trips to a nearby cash-and-carry type outlet.

What you're looking for is a steady supply of good, fresh milk—in the quantities you need. Delivery is a great asset, and becomes even more important as your espresso business grows. The competitive pricing of larger vendors should be factored in, but will have relatively low impact on the ultimate cost per cup. The extra pennies you spend for delivery are generally worth it, and are one way you can contribute to the community by supporting a small, independent business. And *that* usually pays off in unbelievably good service.

Plastic or carton? While cartons are a bit better for the milk itself, plastic jugs are generally more easily recycled. You'll have to make this decision based on availability and your own environmental ethics.

What varieties of milk? The aggressive insistence on a particular fat content, and thus this question of which to offer at the espresso bar, is unique to the United States. Taking an average across the country, whole milk is still the most popular, with nonfat and 2% vying for second place. These breakdowns will give you a good place to start, but in most cases experience is the only way to get a handle on what your consumers want.

Some operators meet the conflict between milk types autocratically, and decide to offer only one middle-of-the road option like 2% or even 1%. In locations where there isn't much competition, such as a sporting arena or on an island ferry, this approach works well.

In other areas, particularly those with a long-standing and sophisticated espresso market, customers become very attached to the flavor qualities of certain types of milk—and their resulting foams. Some espresso operations make a business of giving people exactly what they want. Drinks made of half and half may be among the options requested; this type of beverage is referred to as a "breve." (You can prepare a breve latte, breve cappuccino, breve mocha, etc.)

In some parts of the country, the nondairy latte—itself an oxymoron, given that the English translation of the Italian "latte" is milk—is becoming an obsession. A 50/50 blend of soy and rice milk seems to heat, taste, and look the best. You should be able to locate this product on the shelves of your local health food store; there are wholesalers, but doing volume enough to justify a regular supplier is somewhat inconceivable. (If you can't locate any source for these beverages, offering nondairy alternatives is probably not going to be an issue.)

Using premade chocolate milk is one method of making mochas. It's very convenient, and often provides acceptable quality. Ask your dairy supplier if she produces a chocolate milk, and try it. Look around in your market and see how others are making their mochas. We'll discuss other mocha recipes later.

Finally, there's the icing on the dairy cake. Whipping cream. We said it in the hard goods section, and we'll reiterate here: the canned, prewhipped variety is neither environmentally responsible, practical, nor tasteworthy. Prewhipped cream inevitably spends all of its gas propellant before the canister is empty, which makes for soggy mochas and unnecessary wastage. It increases your supply cost, and comes in a can that has to be thrown in a can. You'll be much happier buying a dispenser, stocking up on chargers, and ordering fresh pint containers as you need them.

FLAVORING SYRUPS

Where syrups are concerned, it's a good idea to keep your selection modest—perhaps around six if you're just using them with coffee, twelve if you plan to offer Italian sodas as well. It is tempting to display all fifty-odd colorful glass bottles, but where? And how confusing for customers!

Keep it simple. Most people will settle for what you have if there is a reasonable selection. Choose about half of your flavors from the nutty, coffee-compatible side of the scale (vanilla, almond, macadamia nut, etc.). The other half, if you are going to make Italian sodas, should represent the fruitier, more exotic side of the spectrum.

Consider a selection from among the following:

For coffee
- almond
- hazelnut

- vanilla
- macadamia nut
- creme de menthe
- Irish creme

For Italian sodas
- kiwi
- raspberry (many mocha drinkers like this in their coffee concoctions, too)
- boysenberry
- passion fruit
- watermelon
- lime

Find a convenient mode of supply. As always, delivery is best. Look for a distributor who sells in mixed cases, which saves you both storage space and money. Consider the cash-and-carry option if your volume will be moderate. Many suppliers will ship these syrups, but freight is expensive and the damage rate is high. You can also seek out plastic bottles, which diminish breakage problems and are becoming increasingly available.

PAPER PRODUCTS

As soon as you decide to get into the espresso business, start looking. You can't find a good supplier too soon. Paper products will be a substantial aspect of your business.

CUPS

The good news is that larger manufacturers—Solo, Sweetheart, Fort Howard, Dixie—are opening their eyes to the possibilities of the hot beverage industry. They're all paying attention to you. Check with a local restaurant supply house, restaurant association, or the Chamber of Commerce to find out when trade shows are planned so you can get a closer look at their products.

Once you've selected a brand, put together a list with the manufacturer and styles of products you want to carry. Send this list out to suppliers in your area to solicit their bids. Depending on the number of suppliers in your area, try to hit at least three. Ascertain their prices, delivery schedule (number of times per week, and which days), minimum delivery requirements, whether their prices include all services and, if you have adequate storage, what quantity discounts are available.

Be aware that custom printing is expensive, and minimum orders are staggering for small operators. Several manufacturers have their own special designs (brown with accents in the color of the Italian flag, for example) for use with espresso; ask specifically about these when you're shopping around.

In the late 1980s, it became very uncool to use Styrofoam hot cups because the material itself implied environmental destruction. Ironically, paper hot cups cause a larger net damage because of the wax, glue, and adhesive used to make them. The incorporation of these materials means there is no way to recycle them. This issue is not as simple as it seems.

At present, there are no recyclable hot cups available on the market. If it concerns you, call manufacturers and environmental groups to research the pros and cons of different options. In all cases, encourage your customers to furnish their own cups by offering them a discount. Five cents per cup is the standard; advertise it.

DOME LIDS

The use of dome lids is a phenomenon unique to the espresso industry. Filling a cup full to the top with an espresso beverage creates a lot of surface tension. Fitting the more traditional flat lid over the top of this beverage prompts a geyser of milk.

Solo Cup Company, Inc. was the first to provide dome lids to the espresso industry. Other manufacturers have since followed suit. We strongly recommend avoiding accidents and spillage by using this type of lid. Make sure it fits the corresponding cup snugly. Sipping spouts makes these lids ideal for commuters.

NAPKINS, STRAWS, SUGAR

Miscellaneous other items are often available directly through your paper supplier. Make sure you're clear about health department restrictions before placing your first order. Do straws need to be wrapped, or presented in a dispenser? Are those wooden stir sticks permissible, or must you choose the less bacteria-prone plastic?

The form in which sugar can be dispensed is often regulated by the health department as well. Using a glass dispenser that pours the sugar out creates the least waste (i.e., less total packaging than individual paper packets), but is not always allowed by health department officials. What kind of sugar should you offer? This depends completely on your market. An old British maxim states, "White with tea, brown with coffee," and although few Americans adhere to that rule, many coffee drinkers prefer raw sugar or honey in their beverages. Survey competitors, and give your preference a try.

Sample Paper Products Bid Sheet

Using a bid sheet is an efficient way to gather the information you need to review your options. The following sample is a convenient format for requesting specific pricing information and terms of service. In addition, by requesting a response, you have placed the ball in your potential supplier's court. Their level of responsiveness should be a telling indicator of their ability and desire to meet your business needs.

September 27, 1996
ABC Paper Co.
555 N. 5th St.
Chicago, IL 60606

Dear Salesperson:

   Mocha Joe's Espresso is opening its first retail outlet in your area. We would appreciate a price quote including terms and conditions of sale on the following items:

- _____ 4-oz. paper hot cups
- _____ 8-oz. paper hot cups
- _____ 12-oz. paper hot cups
- _____ 16-oz. paper hot cups
- _____ "dome" type lids for all cups listed above
- _____ dispenser napkins
- _____ 7" stir sticks

   Please indicate any minimum orders, quantity discounts, order and delivery procedures, etc. Please forward samples and a credit application along with this price quote. Thank you for your prompt response!

Regards,

Joe Monaghan
Purchasing

Recommended Beginning Inventory List

COFFEE

_____ 25 lb. regular beans
_____ 5 lb. decaffeinated beans

MILK

_____ 24 gal. whole or 2%
_____ 8 gal. nonfat

PAPER PRODUCTS

_____ 1 case 4-oz. paper hot cups (1,000/case)
_____ 2 cases each 8-oz. paper hot cups and matching dome lids
_____ 2 cases each 12-oz. paper hot cups and matching dome lids
_____ 1 case each 16-oz. paper hot cups and matching dome lids
_____ Similar denominations of cold cups (clear plastic) and lids if you're planning on a fair amount of iced beverage business
_____ 1 case "stir sticks" or stir straws (7" minimum length)
_____ 12 rolls paper towels
_____ 1 case dispenser napkins (sized to fit your dispenser)

UTENSILS

_____ 3 to 6 milk steaming pitchers (32- to 48-oz.)
_____ 2 milk thermometers with clips for pitchers
_____ Knockbox for used coffee grounds
_____ 4 to 8 shot pitchers or shot glasses
_____ 4 condiment shakers
_____ Pastry display case
_____ Counter brush
_____ 24 pour spouts for use with flavoring syrups
_____ Digital timer for monitoring shots
_____ Whipped cream dispenser with extra chargers
_____ 1 napkin dispenser

SERVEWARE *(for an establishment with seating)*

____ 12 demitasse cups with saucers
____ 4–6 dozen demitasse spoons (definitely optional, but a very nice touch)
____ 2–3 dozen cappuccino cups with saucers
____ 2–3 dozen latte cups or mugs

OTHER SUPPLIES

____ Employee uniforms
____ Paper towels
____ 24 to 48 bar towels
____ 8-qt. plastic bucket
____ 1 gallon bleach for sanitizer
____ Floor mat
____ Floor mop and bucket
____ Pump-type hand soap

MERCHANDISE

(Anything we haven't mentioned that you want to sell alongside your bar, such as insulated mugs, tee-shirts, or packaged chocolates.)

Checklist: Accessories and Renewable Supplies

____ **Define your own starting inventory list, including:**

    ____ Coffee

    ____ Condiments

    ____ Dairy products

    ____ Baked goods/perishables

    ____ Paper products

    ____ Utensils

    ____ Merchandise

    ____ Other

____ **Investigate possible sources for inventory items:**

    —— Mail order supply houses

    —— Local retail and wholesale suppliers

    —— Ongoing suppliers (i.e., your cart supplier may sell utensils)

____ **Send out bid sheets requesting the following:**

    —— Samples

    —— Pricing and conditions of sale

    —— Information about minimum orders and quantity discounts

    —— Order and delivery procedures

____ **Select vendors and establish credit accounts with each to avoid ordering delays**

CHAPTER 10
Determining Your Espresso Menu

Espresso menus around the country look quite similar. The maturity of a market, however, *is* reflected in the arrangement, language, and number of flavored specialties offered. (The newer the market, the more popular are flavored coffees.)

Where the finer points of your menu are concerned, the most important consideration is what's going to sell? The pie charts interspersed among the following pages may shed some light. Ask other local operators what works for them, if they're willing to share information—and many are. Talk with your suppliers to get a feel for the typical product mix. Finally, accept the fact that you're going to have to do some experimenting with your own customers. Keep track of what they're buying; be realistic about what they're not. And don't be shy about asking for feedback.

Espresso Beverages

Keep the coffee menu simple. There's nothing uncomplicated about the way people order their coffee; don't make it worse.

Remember that espresso drinks are handmade. The menu is only a starting point. Baristas create a unique drink for every single person they serve. Let customers know that if they want their cappuccino warmer, cooler, foamier, or just a little heavier on the hazelnut, they shouldn't hesitate to let you know. With a bit of training, your customers will tell you exactly what they want, and how. Your one-on-one service will keep them coming back.

DRINK SIZE

Most espresso menus include prices for three different drink sizes: short (8 ounces), tall (12 ounces), and grande (16 ounces).

TYPICAL SALES MIX BY DRINK SIZE

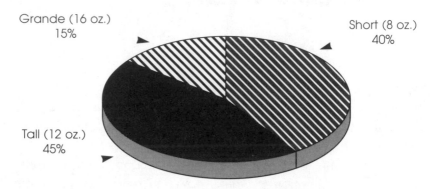

Grande (16 oz.)
15%

Short (8 oz.)
40%

Tall (12 oz.)
45%

Any of these sizes can be made with one or more shots of espresso, and drink recipes call for the addition of varying proportions of milk and steamed milk foam. Straight shots of espresso, of course, measure much less than 8 ounces. The cup in which they are served should be appropriately sized—ideally no larger than 4 ounces.

TYPICAL SALES MIX BY NUMBER OF SHOTS OF ESPRESSO

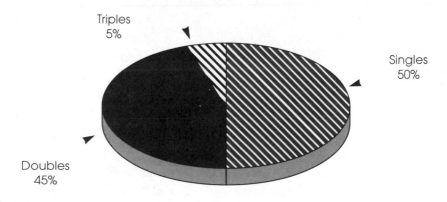

Triples
5%

Singles
50%

Doubles
45%

DRINK VARIETY

On the menu, stay with the five or six most popular drinks—these are, after all, the ones that sell—and add a few creative variations of your own. This will be plenty. A special of the week is a good idea in a cart or deli environment, with a seasonal concoction thrown in when appropriate. In a retail store, specials can complement marketing or merchandising promotions with great success: $.25 off mochas to highlight a new chocolate powder you sell in bulk (the display is nearby, of course), or a free latte with the purchase of any designer porcelain mug.

The six drinks voted most crowd-pleasing are, not necessarily in this order: latte, cappuccino, mocha, espresso, Americano, and hot chocolate.

How do you list these drinks on a menu, and what's needed to concoct them? Pay close attention to the sample menu and recipes on the pages that follow.

TYPICAL SALES MIX BY TYPE OF BEVERAGE

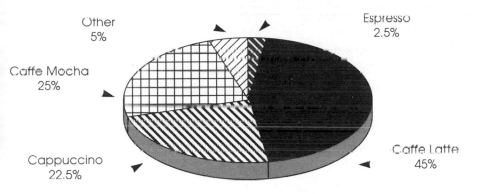

Other 5%

Espresso 2.5%

Caffe Mocha 25%

Caffe Latte 45%

Cappuccino 22.5%

CONDIMENTS

Ask your suppliers what's popular and, again, look around. If you have to submit a plan review for permitting, remember that the health department is going to want to know everything. Be sure to include a condiment run-down in your menu section. A typical condiment list might include the following:

- cocoa powder
- vanilla powder
- ground cinnamon
- nutmeg—this may be powder, but fresh grinders yield pungent taste and add style.
- sugar—white or a combination of this and turbinado, or raw sugar, depending on your market.
- honey
- artificial sweetener—include the pink and the blue. There's no getting around it; people will ask for both.

Make sure your condiment station is placed such that people can stand, shaking liberal cocoa and fooling with their dome lids, without holding up traffic.

Noncoffee Items

ITALIAN SODAS AND JUICES

Very popular among espresso patrons is the Italian soda, a sweet and fizzy mixture of flavored syrup, ice, and soda water (some aficionados add half and half or cream as well). Diehards drink Italian sodas all year round, as will kids coming to the espresso bar with their coffee-loving parents.

While you certainly want to offer an appealing variety, it's better not to offer every single syrup flavor. These come in a wildly exotic spectrum including ginger, chocolate peanut butter, root beer and peach. Try to limit your total inventory to around a dozen, choosing six whose primary purpose is to complement the coffee beverages and six for Italian sodas (see Chapter 9, Accessories and Renewable Supplies).

Bottled water, seltzers, and fresh juice are other popular noncoffee options. Be warned: fresh juice, while it attracts a substantial following among customers, is difficult to handle—especially from a cart—and the health department may not like the idea. Fresh juice requires refrigeration and additional utensils. And the more utensils you use, the more concerned the health department becomes about the risk of contamination.

In addition, you can add a creative plethora of seasonal options to your menu. Both hot spiced cider, for example, and steamed eggnog enjoy a great following in winter weather.

GRANITA

Granita is another Italian invention, and very popular with cart operators in some places. A frozen, slush-type drink, granita is made by combining various flavorings with the fine granita flavor produced by a granita machine. The most common granita flavor may be "coffee"; fresh fruit, and the full range of flavoring syrups, are also used to create refreshing granita varieties. Get creative: you can blend almost anything in a granita machine.

Granita machines tend to be just as expensive as espresso machines, and are historically more prone to mechanical problems. Granita may be just the perfect extension for your espresso business, especially if you're opening an outdoor cart in a warmer climate. But think twice. Find out how profitable granita is in your area, polling carts with locations similar to yours. Make sure you really have the operating space—and market—for the machine before making an investment.

MISCELLANEOUS/FOOD

Offering special food items to complement your espresso beverages is a good idea. The scope of your operation will determine what foodstuffs are appropriate: a restaurant manager may want to spend a little extra time designing desserts and breakfast pastries for his menu, while a cart operator may want to source simpler items like locally made biscotti or individually wrapped chocolates for hers.

There are no sure bets. Trial-and-error is the best form of market research; be nimble. Whether you decide to start out with a host of familiar products, none at all, or try something completely out of the ordinary, keep your ears open and adjust according to customer response. Your goals should be to prevent customers from having to go elsewhere in search of a tasty tidbit, and to promote your image as a full-service espresso bar. Bear in mind that baked goods, particularly, are not a high-profit category. Fresh pastries are highly perishable and therefore easy to waste. Carrying them also means you have to take time to deal with wholesalers.

Where the health department is concerned, the miscellaneous/food category can also prove a bit sticky. Unless you have adequate, permitted or permittable facilities, don't stock anything that needs refrigerating. Feature "dry" pastries—nothing with whipped cream, cream cheese, etc.—and find out exactly what needs to be wrapped individually.

Remember that it's NOT all right to bring baked goods from your home kitchen. If you want to offer treats, find a fresh, local supply of muffins, cookies, scones, biscotti, or other such items. Display them in a countertop case or basket, wrapped individually when necessary. You might want to try wrapped candies, or chocolates on a seasonal basis (these goodies will melt to nothing—bad for business—in the hot sun).

Standard Recipes and Terminology

Espresso Beverages

ESPRESSO

A 1-ounce serving of straight espresso served ungarnished in a small demitasse, 4- or 8-ounce cup. Made to drink immediately, straight espresso should always be fresh. Can also be served as an *espresso macchiato,* with a teaspoon of steamed milk foam, or as an *espresso con pana* with a modest dollop of whipped cream! *Solo* is the Italian word for one, or a single shot of espresso; *doppio* means double, or two shots of espresso.

RISTRETTO

A "restricted" shot of espresso—about 3/4 of a full ounce, the first sweet burst of espresso.

CAPPUCCINO

One ounce of espresso in a cup, topped with equal parts steamed and frothed milk. Named after the fringe of hair ringing the heads of Italy's Capuchin monks. In Italy, the cappuccino is a morning drink— marking the only time Italians take their coffee with milk.

CAFFE LATTE

The latte has a greater proportion of milk than a cappuccino. A 1-ounce serving of espresso, steamed milk up to the top of the cup, and a 1/4" finish of steamed milk foam. Very popular.

CAFFE MOCHA

A 1-ounce serving of espresso poured into a cup holding 1 ounce of chocolate syrup, filled with steamed milk, and topped with a flourish of whipped cream. A very inviting introduction to the world of espresso!

AMERICANO

"Americanized" espresso: 1 or more servings of espresso (the ratio for the menu should be your call, a matter of taste) diluted (hot water) to the strength of drip coffee. Dark, fresh, intense.

CAFFE BREVE

A latte made not with steamed milk, but instead by adding rich, steamed half and half.

Iced Espresso Drinks

The most important guideline for making iced drinks is to use cold milk. You may laugh, but there are baristas who will steam the milk before pouring it over ice. That's a sure way to turn your clientele away. Another tip: To make an iced mocha with chocolate syrup instead of premixed chocolate milk, stir the hot espresso and chocolate syrup together thoroughly before adding cold milk. Ice comes last, and whipped cream is optional.

Add-Ons

FLAVORING

Start with less—you can always add more. Flavor any drink by covering the bottom of the cup with syrup, and then continuing to make the drink by the book.

EXTRA SHOTS

Often called "doubles" or "triples" based on the total number of shots in the drink, extra shots should be added upon request. A double shot of espresso measures 2 full ounces; a triple calls for 3 full ounces, and so on.

Noncoffee Beverages

STEAMED MILK, WITH OR WITHOUT FLAVORING

Just like it sounds—milk steamed, the appropriate flavoring added (directions for flavoring are above; pricing is below).

HOT COCOA

One ounce of chocolate syrup with steamed milk (go easy on the heat for kids), whipped cream on top.

ITALIAN SODA

One ounce of flavored syrup combined with mineral water or club soda (adding half and half makes an extra thick treat). The flavoring and mineral water together are a refreshing and low-calorie drink.

PRICING

Pricing is tough when you're just starting out. Take a look at the average highs and lows for 8-ounce drinks listed below, then shop. What price range will your market and particular location support? What kind of a markup do you need to realize worthwhile profit? Trust your intuition.

Espresso: $.75–1.50

Caffe Latte: $1.00–2.00

Cappuccino: $1.00–2.00

Caffe Mocha: $1.50–2.00

Flavoring: $.25–.50

Extra shot in any drink: $.25–.75

These standards and recipes will provide a good base for developing the menu on your cart. Keep in mind, however, that the keys to pleasing customers are dedication and customization. Make each drink well, just the way your coffee-loving customer wants it!

Sample Menu

	1 oz.	2 oz.
ESPRESSO	$1.00	$1.50

Strong, intense brew served straight

	8 oz.	12 oz.	16 oz.
CAFFE LATTE	$1.35	$1.65	$1.95

Espresso and steamed milk, topped with froth

CAPPUCCINO	$1.35	$1.65	$1.95

Espresso with equal parts steamed and frothed milk

CAFFE MOCHA	$1.60	$1.90	$2.20

Espresso with steamed hot chocolate, topped with whipped cream

Flavors (in any drink)   add $0.25

Almond, Hazelnut, Vanilla

Double Shot (in any drink)   add $0.50

Pastries baked fresh daily • Prices and selection vary

Checklist: Determining Your Menu

___ **Assess your market**

    ___ Determine what's selling in your area and how much it costs

    ___ Brainstorm ways to set your menu apart, if possible (NOTE: The quality of your drinks alone may be a distinguishing factor!)

___ **Build your espresso menu**

    ___ Decide on the basics, including:

        ___ Core drinks (and drink recipes)

        ___ Sizes

        ___ Basic drink prices

    ___ Plan add-ons, including:

        ___ Flavors and flourishes (i.e., extra whipped cream)

        ___ Extra shots

        ___ Pricing for these

    ___ Devise a few variations or seasonal specialties

___ **Add non-coffee beverages, considering:**

    ___ Logical outgrowths of your coffee beverages, such as steamed milk and hot chocolate

    ___ Italian sodas

    ___ Fresh juices

    ___ Granita

___ **Consider including fresh or packaged food items that complement your coffee menu**

___ **Consult your records and your staff to see if the menu needs modification based on cost or customer response**

CHAPTER 11
Investing in Personnel

In Italy, the position of the *barista,* or espresso bartender, is a prestigious one. Most espresso bars are owner-operated and family-run, practicing an extremely hands-on management philosophy. Espresso is a career. The espresso scene in the United States, on the other hand, tends to be associated with fast food. Most baristas—often students on their way to something else—are paid low wages.

The choice is yours. What happens in a business where employees are paid well and given meaningful responsibility, thorough training, and superior equipment with which to work? Success. Consider giving your baristas everything they need to take pride in their work, making the very best drinks and giving outstanding service to you and your valuable customers.

Hiring

People frequent espresso bars as much for the purchasing experience as for the drink itself. If you are planning to be a barista in your espresso business, do a quick double-check: do I have the energy and the outgoing, friendly personality that will make this a success? If you choose to hire or train other employees, screen them carefully for the same characteristics.

There are three main qualities you'll want to look for in a prospective barista. For the most part, these reflect the same kind of common sense approach you'd want to use when hiring for any business. Because espresso is such an intensely hands-on product, however, and barista-customer relationships are so crucial to success, you'll feel the impact of your decisions with force. Give each of these qualities equal weight. Take the extra time needed to check references, and trust your intuition.

Personality. To build a steady customer base, the person behind the espresso machine needs to be gregarious, friendly, and fun. A good memory for names and faces is a plus; the barista who remembers his customers' drinks is a hit. Customers return to him. Look for someone who is not afraid to attract attention, make jokes, call out. Most of all, you want someone who is courteous and infinitely likable.

It's not always easy to find someone who will give as much of themselves from behind the bar as you would yourself. Incentives will help; consider bonuses based on monthly sales or specific shift revenues, added responsibility such as inventory and ordering duties, or merit-based raises with a pre-established system of measurement.

Coordination. Frankly, there is nothing worse than a clumsy barista. A barista must inspire the confidence and trust of his customers. And you, of course, want to keep hot water related accidents to the absolute minimum.

Although espresso systems are becoming increasingly automated, there is still no substitute for the ability to create a great espresso drink. Your espresso operators should be detail-oriented and quick, with admirable manual dexterity. Prior food service experience will help your employee manage the details. Look for employees who enjoy—and can maintain—a high learning curve.

Reliability. Finally and fundamentally, your employees should be honest. In the crudest of terms, you want someone who will show up on time and not steal. Recommendations and references are invaluable. Look for someone who will share your desire to deliver a quality product, and follow through on it. For an espresso operation, the risk of internal stealing can be quite high.

Especially in a mobile or cart operation where your barista doubles as the cashier, opportunities to pocket latte money are frequent. In addition to checking references, there are two primary ways to guard against theft: know your business, and be honest with your employees about your expectations.

If you've worked the bar yourself and know when high-volume times are likely to hit—and about how much revenue they'll yield—you should have a pretty good instinct for inconsistencies. Expect the best, but be alert to sudden or steady dips in profit. Watch for patterns. For greater inventory control, some espresso cart owners "issue" cups to their employees at the beginning of each shift. Employees are responsible for a dollar amount that is at least as high as the number of cups missing; goodies and personal cups should elevate the cash even more.

If you don't already have this dependable and skillful staff, you may find yourself needing one. Network with others in the specialty coffee or food service industry; someone may know of a good employee seeking hours. Advertise locally with flyers or announcements, and perhaps in the city paper. Spread the word among the organizations—academic or recreational, religious or sports-oriented—with which you have contact.

Don't worry that just because you're opening in a brand new market, you'll have no hiring luck. True, new market work forces rarely feature trained baristas. Mature markets, however, often feature an abundance of individuals trained to practice terrible habits. Which leads us to the next personnel topic: the importance of good training.

The Importance of Good Training

When you're striving for quality from employees, proper training is essential. New baristas need to be comprehensively trained to operate all equipment and to prepare superlative beverages according to standard. They must also be schooled to offer flawless customer service, for it is this excellence of service in combination with the custom product of espresso that enables you to charge premium prices.

Regardless of the training format you choose, make it consistent from employee to employee. At the very least, organize the topics you want to cover in the form of a typed outline and present that outline to your trainees. You may want to purchase prepared training tools, particularly for the espresso-specific content of the training. (Appendix A lists several books and videotapes that are useful during training.)

There is also a growing number of consultants out there, specializing in both training and coffee. Ask around. Some of these consultants set up seminars in their own towns, while others will travel to your site for a fee plus expenses. Make sure you gain access to any training expertise your equipment and coffee suppliers have to offer as well. Many will design custom sessions for your staff, and although the level of effectiveness does vary, they're often very good.

Make sure customers view your business as a cohesive entity, and the employees as a working team. Prepare your employees to impress the public with a high level of coffee knowledge—but politely, and with humility. Use training as a tool to further these goals, while establishing good interpersonnel communication. An effective training tells employees: This is who we are. This is what we do. This is why we do it. And here's where you can go when you need something in order to do your job better.

Training curricula should cover the following subject areas:

Product knowledge. Communicate with employees about how deliberately you chose the fine equipment, fabulous coffee, and mouth-watering baked goods you did. They'll pass the information along to customers, adding credibility to your reputation for producing a great product. Make sure each employee can answer questions about ingredients and flavorings. (Someone always asks if the brownies have nuts.)

Where bar skills are concerned, every employee should be thoroughly trained in preparation for opening day. If at all possible, get them on the bar for good, solid practice well in advance—as much as you can. Baristas hired subsequent to opening day should have a full two weeks of training, on-site and during work hours, before being left to make drinks on their own. Include drink standards and preparation, food serving etiquette, and cash handling.

Company values. During working hours, your employees represent your company's identity. They should be able to describe it. This identity is your point of differentiation, the excellence and charisma that draw coffee lovers to your side of the street. Each member of your staff should be articulate about the values the company espouses

A document explaining your company's values, guiding principles, and goals is a document worth having. Look back to your business plan for clarity: What do you want for your business? What are your personal standards? What are your product standards? What kind of a model for interaction with customers do you want to establish? Share this document with employees as they begin their tenure with your company.

Employment policy. Your employment policy may be as simple as a piece of paper with your logo on it which spells out company policies, the customer service ethic you expect, and possible reasons for termination. Find out what's legal, what you really can and want to require. Include daily dress requirements; espres-so is very messy, so you may want to consider some type of uniform or dark apron for everyone behind the counter. Remember to list applicable food handling and health codes. Stress good hygiene.

This policy is a strategic and effective place to enumerate the more intangible expectations you have of your employees, such as making customers feel welcome. Without writing such expectations in this document, there is no way you can legally hold employees responsible. With a signed copy, you can terminate an employee if the contract is not fulfilled. Have each employee sign this policy, and make sure you keep a copy on file.

Should the employee policy really be part of training? You bet. While you may want to go over the policy individually with each new hire, your formal training program is the perfect place to discuss specific expectations. *Your employees communicate the identity of your business.* What you spell out in your employee policy is an important part of what you need to train employees to do. And if you are training more than one employee, the peer pressure activated by talking about these issues in a group will work in your favor.

Job Descriptions

It is vital that everyone who works with your business shares an understanding of who does what. If roles are fuzzy, something won't get done. "Something" usually turns into a lot of things, which have a tendency to snowball before they're uncovered. And unless you are extremely lucky, one of these things will be uncovered by the health department, a customer, or yourself— late at night, balancing the books just before taxes are due.

So define job descriptions clearly. The hierarchy of a cart operation, for example, might look something like the diagram on page 136.

Your Operations Manual

In addition to providing a clear employee policy and job descriptions, we urge you not to underestimate the importance of an operations manual. An operations manual functions some-what like a guide book. In your absence—even if you're just at the other end of the counter, but busy with a customer—the operations manual will give your employees the information they need to do things precisely the way you'd like them to be done.

Sample Employee Policy

This sample represents the simplest possible form of employee policy. You may want to expand the scope of yours to include issues such as vacation pay, holidays, sick leave, overtime practices, health issues or employee civil rights.

As an employee of Mocha Joe's espresso catering, I agree to:

- Show up for work at the scheduled time, and at least 10 minutes before the start of a bar shift.

- Dress appropriately: Clean Mocha Joe's t-shirt, jeans, khakis or neutral-colored skirt, closed-toe shoes.

- Maintain a polite and professional demeanor when representing Mocha Joe's by working the cart, interacting with customers or industry associates, and whenever wearing a Mocha Joe's uniform in public.

- Take responsibility for keeping my Multnomah County food handler's permit valid and furnishing Mocha Joe's with an up-to-date copy.

- Exercise caution and care with dangerous materials (i.e., electrical equipment, hot liquids, etc.).

- Produce a high-quality product at all times concerning drink preparation, cart and product presentation, and cleanliness standards.

I understand that failing to subscribe to any one of these policies may result in immediate termination.

_____   _____
Employee's Signature   Date

Basic Job Descriptions: Espresso Cart

Even the most general job descriptions will get you started off on the right foot. Be flexible, but be clear. And if you start out as a one-person show, don't worry—just plug your own name in everywhere (and take a hot bath at the end of the day). In due course and with ample growth, your name will be replaced with others.

Owner

As King or Queen of the cart, your job is to establish a vision for the business. Set reasonable but impelling goals, chart strategic direction, and keep your finger on the funds to make sure the business is thriving in the way you need and want it to. If not, reroute. Managing the big picture is your responsibility.

Manager

If you aren't the manager of your business, find someone as trustworthy and dependable as you are to do so. The manager's job description is a tall order: scheduling, sales and cash reconciliation, the daily book routine, bank deposits, equipment maintenance, inventory control and ordering.

Baristas

The baristas are your business' public relations team. They prepare drinks, provide customer service, maintain company policies, create general ambiance, and handle the opening, closing, and cleaning of the espresso operation.

In addition, an operations manual empowers employees to use resources and find solutions. Employees with these attributes will be the most successful, and affect your business in the most positive way. There are prewritten versions available, but experience shows that the operations manual will be more effective in the long run if you've assembled it yourself.

The table of contents for a thorough operations manual should look something like this:

I. Beverage standards

    A. Recipes

    B. Preparation and product handling

    C. Presentation

II. Opening procedures

    A. Coffee

    B. Milk

    C. Paper products and dishware

    D. Pastries

III. Operating Procedures

    A. Quality control

    B. Cleaning and restocking

    C. Ordering

IV. Closing Procedures

    A. Equipment maintenance/cleaning

    B. Coffee storage

    C. Cleaning of facility

Other business-related but equally important items that should be included are procedures for handling inventory, cash transactions, and bookkeeping.

Checklist: Investing in Personnel

____ **Define job descriptions**

    ____ Titles and duties.

    ____ Salary

    ____ Organizational hierarchy (who reports to whom)

____ **Write an employee policy, including expectations regarding:**

    ____ Timeliness and appropriate dress

    ____ Attitude on-the-job, with customers and co-workers

    ____ Individual licensing requirements

    ____ Safety issues

    ____ General product quality standards

____ **Outline your training program**

    ____ Product knowledge

    ____ Company values

    ____ Employment policies

____ **Assemble your operations manual, including:**

    ____ Beverage standards

    ____ Operating procedures

    ____ Opening and closing procedures

    ____ Inventory guidelines

    ____ Handling cash transactions

    ____ Bookkeeping protocol

____ **Publicize the fact that you're hiring**

____ **Interview and make hiring decisions**

____ **Schedule and implement new employee training**

CHAPTER 12
Ensuring Espresso
Drink Quality

This chapter is meant to serve both as an introduction to brewing techniques, and as an ongoing reference. If you've not yet pulled your first shot of espresso, some of the information presented may be confusing. Hang in there. Read this chapter carefully, and come back to it after you pull your first solo. Re-read the pages after you've pulled your 20th shot, your 70th, and again after your 270th.

The more experience you gain, the more meaningful the tips will become. As a seasoned barista, you will be better able to apply them. As a manager, plan to incorporate those you find most valuable into the training sessions you structure for employees. Note that we haven't attempted to cover everything: the majority of your espresso bar training, including lots of hands-on practice, should come from your espresso machine and coffee suppliers.

We begin with milk handling because, chronologically, milk is the barista's first consideration when faced with a drink order. Steamed milk holds its heat and texture far longer than a fresh shot of espresso, which must be used in a drink within seconds. A skillful barista receives an order, checks his milk situation, and begins to steam or foam if necessary. It is only after he knows the milk supply is adequate that he turns to brew his espresso.

Milk Handling

Steaming milk, which is typically done in a steaming pitcher, involves using the tip of the espresso machine's steam wand to inject steam into the liquid. Proper milk steaming is achieved by balancing the tip of the steam wand on the milk's surface. This process simultaneously heats and aerates the milk, producing a mixture of hot milk and creamy foam.

The ability to manipulate this mixture of milk and foam is the secret to preparing the full menu of espresso drinks correctly. Skillful milk handling also enables the barista to satisfy the special requests and drink preferences of her customers.

The basic steps of steaming and foaming milk are as follows:

- Fill your steaming pitcher half full with cold milk.

- Insert the tip of your steaming wand just below the milk's surface, then open the steam valve all the way for a full flow of steam. Lower the pitcher to balance the tip of the steam wand on the surface of the milk.

- When the desired amount of foam is created, submerse the wand deep into the milk until your thermometer reads just above 150°F.

- Quickly shut off the flow of steam and remove the pitcher.

- Clean your steam wand with a wet rag and a few short bursts of steam.

Let's take a closer look at each step.

Fill your steaming pitcher half full with cold milk. Always use a stainless steel steaming pitcher. Never start with your pitcher more than half full of milk. Have faith; it will grow.

Insert the tip of your steaming wand just below the milk's surface. When the wand is all the way under, open the steam valve all the way for a full flow of steam. Position your pitcher so that the tip of the steam wand is balanced on the surface of the milk. This is a delicate place, and finding it is simply a matter of time and experience.

The milk shouldn't spurt or sputter, but should instead roll under the tip of the wand. After a moment, it should begin to spin in circles. Listen for a gentle sucking sound as air is pulled into the milk. Avoid excess movement of the pitcher, either up and down or around and around. Novices do it all the time, but that exaggerated movement makes for overly aerated foam: big, short-lived bubbles and altogether inferior texture.

When the desired amount of foam is created, submerse the wand deep into the milk. Keep it there until your thermometer reads just above 150°F. Here's where your thermometer earns its keep. For the best taste, steam milk to a temperature of about 150–160°F. Like humans, milk is basically organic and starts to scald around 180°F.

Quickly shut off the flow of steam and remove the pitcher. A word of caution: the wand is hot. Even with direct contact, the steam itself won't usually burn you. The wand will.

When pouring drinks, use your large spoon or spatula to hold back foam, then push it forward. As a general rule, don't spoon the foam into the drink. Frankly, it's amateurish, and just doesn't make as nice a drink. But if your customer wants a "dry cappuccino"—one in which the milk content is supposed to be purely made up of foam—you should feel free to use your spoon to do exactly that.

Some polished baristas can segregate the milk from the foam completely with an expert shake of the wrist. This, too, comes with time. Experiment with pouring slowly for hot milk (the foam will hold back), and more quickly when you want a greater ratio of foam (making a cappuccino, for example).

Clean your steam wand with a wet rag and a few short bursts of steam. Unless traffic is constant, refrigerate the pitcher and its residual milk. Before resteaming, add at least half again as much fresh milk—without exceeding the half-full rule. Be vigilant about making sure enough fresh milk is added. Customers will notice if you aren't; old, oversteamed milk tastes horrible. Finally, clean that steam wand every single time you use it.

And practice.

Brewing Espresso

There's no way to get around it: pulling a good shot of espresso is still the key to making a good espresso drink. No matter how much milk or flavoring is added, espresso is still the heart of the operation. And understanding the importance of espresso quality is the first big step toward achieving it.

An acceptable shot of espresso is made with 7 grams of great coffee (in most cases, espresso blend), freshly and finely ground. That espresso is packed tightly and brewed with 1 to 1–1/2 ounces of hot, high-pressure water for a total of 18–24 seconds.

To brew good espresso:

- Dose the appropriate amount of espresso from the grinder into your portafilter.

- Tamp grounds firmly so the grounds will hold onto the brewing water, or "extract," for the appropriate amount of time.

- Fit your portafilter snugly into the espresso machine group.

- Brew.

- Empty the portafilter, rinse it, and replace.

Again, let's take a closer look:

Dose the appropriate amount of espresso from the grinder into your portafilter. The coffee must be ground to the right fineness or coarseness, so that the most desirable flavor characteristics are extracted from the coffee. The range of grind that yields these flavors is extraordinarily narrow.

Dosing is the act of measuring coffee out of a doser or grinder—or, heaven forbid, manually spooning the coffee—into a portafilter. The doser should be set, preferably by your machine supplier, to dose consistently. A word of coffee-dosing caution: if a coffee roaster tells you his coffee will save you money because it's so good that less is required for brewing, heads up. This is never the case.

The Fundamentals of Brewing Espresso

Understanding the importance of brewing quality espresso is the first step towards achieving it. An acceptable shot of espresso is made with 7 grams of superb espresso, freshly and finely ground. That espresso is packed tightly and brewed with 1 to 1–1/2 ounces of hot, high-pressure water for about 18–24 seconds.

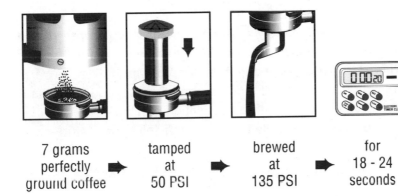

| 7 grams perfectly ground coffee | ➡ | tamped at 50 PSI | ➡ | brewed at 135 PSI | ➡ | for 18 - 24 seconds |

—1 oz.

=

The perfect
shot of
espresso

Make sure, when you dose, that there is enough coffee to cover the pie-shaped wedges at the bottom of the chamber. Ideally, the chamber should be kept half-full of ground coffee; but never grind more espresso coffee than can be used in one hour.

Be aggressive when you pull the dosing handle. Coffee is very moist, and you may not get a full dose unless you're determined to make it happen. Avoid half-dosing. This sets you up for an inadequate dose the next time around, and you'll lose stray grounds out the bottom of the doser.

Tamp grounds firmly so the grounds will hold onto the brewing water, or "extract," for the appropriate amount of time. When tamping, place the base of your portafilter on a solid surface. (This can mar your countertop, so you may want to prepare the surface with an insulating mat or steel plate.) Using a hand tamper, put plenty of oomph into your tamp—a good hard pack usually falls somewhere close to the optimal 50 pounds per square inch—and give a firm twist to even out the grounds. A light, delicate tamp necessitates a finer grind to create the same amount of resistance, and this fine grind tends to clog holds in the portafilter and diffusing screens.

Some baristas like to tap the edge of the portafilter with the edge of their tamper to loosen stray grinds; then they give the coffee another light tamp. Feel free to customize the specifics, but develop a tamping style that's consistent.

Fit your portafilter snugly into the espresso machine group. It's a good idea to lightly sweep ground coffee off the rim of your portafilter before placing it in the group of the machine. This extra step saves long-term wear and tear on group gaskets.

Once the portafilter is placed in the group, brewing must begin within 15 seconds. Otherwise, the coffee begins to deteriorate. Don't let heat and moisture steal coffee freshness! Fresh, finely ground coffee is ripe to give the best it's got and it will, even if you're not ready to take advantage of it. Begin brewing immediately after the portafilter is placed up in the machine group casting.

Brew. Ideal brewing temperature is around 195°–197°F, and ideal pressure—the trademark of the espresso method of brewing—is 9 atmospheres of pressure, or about 130 psi.

Whether you do it manually or automatically, run 1 to 1–1/2 ounces of water through the espresso for every 7-gram measure or "shot." Less than one ounce can be fine, but the resulting espresso may lack fullness and not carry its taste through a quantity of milk.

Use more than 1–1/2 and you run the risk of over-extraction and bitterness. If your machine is an automatic, the press of a button will be enough to command the right volume of water. If your machine is a semi-automatic, you will have to stop the flow manually, using your shot glass or timer as a gauge.

As we pointed out above, the ideal brewing time for espresso is 18–24 seconds. Any longer, and the espresso will be "overextracted"—burnt-tasting, astringent, and bitter because the sugars have deteriorated. Shorter, and it's "underextracted"— light in body with pale crema, insipid and sour.

Whenever possible, brew espresso into the cup in which it is to be served. As we emphasized previously, this practice saves valuable crema.

Use all shots of espresso within 10–15 seconds. When coffee is brewed—and thereby exposed to excess temperature and water—its best stuff dissipates rapidly. If you don't put it to use immediately, it's gone. Remember: quality is the key. Don't be tempted to salvage $.25 worth of coffee at the risk of alienating your customer with a bad drink.

Empty the portafilter, rinse it, and replace. Keep your portafilters in the groups when they're not in use; this keeps them warm, which makes for significantly better coffee. The keen-eyed, quality-conscious customer will veer sharply out of line at the sight of a portafilter lying on the drain tray or counter.

Keep your espresso machine clean. A dirty machine *can't* brew good coffee. Brewing through coffee residue is like using the same grounds over and over again. Would you do that at home?

More to the point, would you pay $2.00 to have someone else do it for you? (See Chapter 14, Equipment Maintenance, for cleaning guidelines.)

General Coffee Freshness Tips

• Whole bean coffee should be used within a week of its exposure to air, and never beyond 10–14 days. Depending on the type of packaging used, the "death date" could be one week from the day of roasting or from the day coffee is sealed in its vacuum-locked packaging.

• Once exposed, coffee should be protected from air, light, heat, and moisture. Ask your roaster to review storage options with you.

• If you keep your beans in bins or drawers, wipe them out between batches. Use a clean, dry cloth (cotton bar towels are ideal)—no moisture or soap. Any dampness will sap coffee flavor, while soap residue will taint it.

• Never mix stale beans with fresh. It takes about 50 beans to brew a good shot of espresso, and only one bad one to ruin it.

• Never put more beans in the cone-shaped hopper of your espresso grinder than can be used within 8 hours.

• Use ground espresso within one hour. During notably slow periods, turn off the automatic timer on your grinder (if you have one) so you can keep coffee grinding moderate.

Checklist: Ensuring Espresso Quality

____ **Handle milk expertly**

____ Steam using a steaming pitcher made of stainless steel

____ Whenever possible, begin with cold milk

____ While steaming, avoid excess movement of the pitcher

____ Always steam milk to between 150° and 160°F, and serve it that way!

____ Keep steamed milk in refrigerator when not in use

____ Before resteaming, double volume with fresh, cold milk

____ Keep steam wand clean

____ **Brew espresso flawlessly**

____ Use ground espresso within one hour

____ Make sure dosing chamber is full enough to dispense an appropriate dose, and avoid half-dosing

____ Tamp with adequate force (50 p.s.i.)

____ Brew within 15 seconds of placing portafilter in group

____ Keep an eye on the fundamentals: 7 grams coffee per shot, brewed with 1 to 1-1/2 ounces water, in 18–24 seconds

____ Adjust grind as necessary to achieve correct brewing time

____ Whenever possible, brew directly into serving container

____ Use brewed shots of espresso *immediately*

____ Keep espresso machine clean

____ **Prepare and present drinks with care**

____ Follow drink recipes consistently, except when catering to individual customer requests

____ Serve a neat-looking and excellent-tasting drink every time

CHAPTER 13
Marketing Your
Espresso Operation

The task now before you is to spread the word. The essence of marketing your business is to determine the ways in which you can make it appealing and accessible to a large customer base.

The Creative Approach

Marketing espresso through conventional means is expensive and can be frustratingly difficult. There are few if any traditional programs that provide useful support for smaller mobile-type operations. In general, marketing to commuters and foot traffic is tough. They're all coming from different places, and it's hard to find a medium— aside from your own storefront— that reaches a large block of them.

Adding espresso to an existing restaurant or retail business is easier because in most cases both clientele and advertising venues already exist. In all cases, the key is to gain as much visibility as you possibly can.

On the following pages, you'll find low-cost advertising suggestions geared toward doing exactly that. Experiment. Every location is different. Given time and dollars, your efforts will encourage the growth of the business. Good options include:

- Printing and distributing flyers that feature a freebie of one kind or another.

- Stamping "good for one free espresso beverage of your choice" on the back of your business cards (you should have them by now) and carry them with you at all times. Hand them out at social events, business meetings, sporting events, and any time you run into someone you think might be interested in a good drink.

- Advertising in a local, in-house newsletter.

- Hanging a banner—for a maximum of two weeks, after which time no one will notice it—that announces a grand opening special (before you do this, make sure there are no lease restrictions on this kind of display). If the banner isn't an option, try for a sidewalk sandwich board.

You might also want to try:

- Advertising a "Happy Hour," offering a discount on drinks during one of your slower times.

- Printing punch cards to encourage regular business (some operators even keep them in a card box on the counter so customers don't have to carry them around).

- Establishing a "pre-pay" program. Invite customers to pay for one month's lattes in advance (about $60.00). You keep track of their purchases with a rubber stamp indicating the day's date and an index card with your customer's name and balance on it. You gain added flexibility (read: cash flow), and your customer gets terrific convenience.

- Listing specials of the day or week on your menu (inspiring customers to experiment with a new flavor or creative concoction is a great way to promote higher-priced, add-on type drinks).

- Offering seasonal specialties.

- Featuring a commuter program by selling a mug with your logo and offering a discount to anyone who brings their mug in for a fill-up.

- Selling an in-car cup holder, t-shirt, baseball cap, pin, or magnet with your name and logo.

Sample Marketing Materials

Collateral materials such as flyers and punch cards help boost general awareness and customer loyalty.

Espresso
Catering

Let **Mocha Joe's Espresso Catering** bring an espresso bar to your next party, business meeting or sporting event! Mocha Joe's is the best choice for espresso catering, 100% satisfaction guaranteed! We provide:

Professional Staff
Our courteous staff will arrive promptly, set up efficiently and serve on time. Style, speed, just the right amount of personality—and we don't leave a trace.

The Best Espresso Equipment
Our wide variety of espresso equipment gives us the versatility to serve the highest quality beverages anywhere! We can handle event sizes from 40 to 4,000 persons.

The Best Ingredients
We use only top quality ingredients, including Starbucks Coffee and Da Vinci Gourmet Syrups, in order to provide your guests with the finest beverages.

Please call for our affordable rates & glowing references.

(206) 555-8848

Mocha Joe's
Espresso

(206) 555-8848

Actually paying for advertising is not always a good use of the budget. Especially where carts are concerned, customers don't want to shop around. They're looking for convenience and quality. What you *can* do is create a name for yourself. Use large, colorful signage—consider neon, if it's allowed—and mark your condiment containers and menu with graphics that match.

Get involved in the community to increase visibility and stimulate more good will. Provide matching employee walk-a-thon uniforms with your name and logo or colors. Consider paying for sponsorships or making other similar "donations." Here are a couple of ideas to get you started:

- Serve espresso at a foot race or other public athletic event.

- Donate a gift certificate to a benefit auction or other fundraising event (public radio membership drive, for example) in exchange for a description of your services during the actual bidding.

- Sponsor a little league team in your area—make sure your logo is across the back of their uniforms, and distribute coupons for hot chocolate and espresso at the games.

- Target one local office group a week, delivering a menu and a coupon for each employee.

Finally, make sure the espresso business itself leaves a good impression. Brew great drinks, create an upbeat and positive experience, be professional and dependable. More specifically, try this:

- Welcome customers by making certain that your menu and pricing are straightforward and easy to understand.

- Clean, clean, clean! Keep your business spotless. This includes the building, equipment, and staff. In your establishment, there is no such thing as an idle barista. First impressions are critical, and the appearance of your business is a primary determining factor.

- Avoid clutter. This is an ongoing challenge, particularly with a cart operation. Assign each utensil and supply its own place, and keep it there. Avoid frequent rearrangement of condiments, napkins, lids, etc. Customers like consistency.

• Perform frequent evaluations of your business' appearance. Be consistent in the format of these evaluations, perhaps using a simple form to help you scrutinize the finest details. Are there old coffee grounds under the espresso machine, where they're visible to the customer? Milk splatter on the sneeze guard? Is the bean hopper on your grinder clean and free of past coffee oils?

• Prompt your customers frequently for honest and candid feedback. Be open to criticism; never take a defensive attitude. Let them know you are genuinely interested in their opinions, and reward participation with a free drink every now and then.

These are your most persuasive marketing tools, and they're comparatively inexpensive. Use them!

Good Public Relations

Public relations, or P.R., is defined as a means for using any form of media—print, radio or television—to gain positive recognition for a person, place or thing. When we talk about P.R., we are talking about getting to know the journalists in your area and, by presenting them with compelling story ideas that are more or less tied into your business or clientele, increasing awareness and winning media coverage. In this section, we want to stimulate your thinking about all of the ways you can make P.R. pay off for your business.

The issue of good P.R. pops up in many areas. When you smile at your customer as you hand her a latte, you are "doing good P.R." If you donate coffee to the annual zoo fundraising banquet, you're doing good P.R. Every time you interact with the public as a representative of your company and engender good will in these ways, you contribute to the growth of your business.

Take the concept a step further. You know it's a thrill to see your name in print, in a local newspaper or newsletter. But have you ever stopped to think how many potential customers are reading the same page? Many. And because the editorial or photo with your name is not part of a paid advertisement, it sends an especially strong and useful message.

Anyone with money can take out an ad. Just about every ad claims that its sponsor offers the biggest, best, or most economical products. But a mention in a news article carries weight. Consumers assume that reporters are more critical than whoever runs the classified section. Getting your name in unpaid print gives you an extra measure of credibility with the public, and is usually read by substantially more people.

Getting your name and photo in the *Sunnyside News* is a lot like sending a smile over the top of that latte. But the *Sunnyside News* reaches more people, and faster. It also stays around longer and—unlike a flyer or an ad—it's free.

DOING YOUR HOMEWORK

Regardless of scale, the media push you plan will be much more effective if you've done your homework up front. When we say homework, here's what we mean:

Take the time to understand your own business. Make sure you can articulate what's special about it. What is your purpose, and what services do you provide? What do you offer that is unique, either in terms of service, or expertise, or business approach? What are you doing that no one else is? What is notable or intriguing about your background? How did you get into this business after all? Who are your customers, and what kind of relationships do you have with them?

Become familiar with regional publications and the journalists who write for them. Keeping an eye on the editors listed on the masthead doesn't hurt, either. Compile a list of the business, food, and feature writers in your daily and weekly newspapers.

Scan area magazines and newsletters for places your stories might be a great "fit." Make contact with any journalists and editors you think would be interested in your business; send them information about your operation, relevant activities, and the coffee industry as a whole. Be liberal as you reach out, but do discriminate. Use your own judgement to decide whether or not the information you're sending is appropriate. If in doubt, call and ask. Most journalists have a good feel for their subject area and will tell you whether or not you fit in it. As you get to know them, ask your writing contacts for leads—who else might be interested in your story?

Come up with story ideas to pitch to the press. Journalists have readers to please, too. Send them something they can use and they'll appreciate you for it. Brainstorm for ideas with colleagues or friends. This list may help you get started:

- **New business.** If you're just starting a new operation, introduce yourself. Business journals exist, in part, to publicize openings like yours. Just send a press release that discusses the principle figures in your company, your mission, the services you'll provide and, if relevant, your company philosophy. Remember to include anything that is special or different about what you're doing.

- **New contracts/services.** Pitch a story about new contracts you have with existing or new businesses in your area. This should go to local trade or business journals. Promote changes in the services you offer. Offering a new line of syrups? Serving as part of a Rose Bowl experiment to sell espresso instead of beer?

- **New partnerships.** Both mainstream publications and trade journals love stories about unique business partnerships. If you help a small non-profit get on its feet, for example, talk about it. If you work with a group of students to get a student-run espresso joint going on campus, spread the word about that.

- **Trainings and tastings.** Education is a big draw, and so is free espresso. Holding a fun and informational tasting or espresso training class is a great way to bring journalists into your operation. Spending time on your turf, they get a first-hand impression of your business and what you have to offer. They'll take away a new respect for the espresso industry, will feel pleasure at having steamed milk or brewed a shot, and will tell their readers all about you.

- **Seminars for food groups.** As a coffee expert, you have much to offer local food groups such as culinary associations and fine food clubs. Develop informational seminars on topics like wine and coffee pairings, complementary coffee and foods—or just how to brew a great cup of coffee or shot of espresso. Consider working with a local food guru to draw a more diverse crowd. The tie-in also gives your event a better chance of being picked up by the press.

WRITING A PRESS RELEASE

The press release is the most widely used tool in public relations (O.K., the smile ranks first), and is typically well received and understood by journalists. A good press release is focused and succinct, and offers a streamlined version of your story.

The press release opens with a captivating headline and opening paragraph that "hooks" writers into calling you for the details. When you put your release together, try to take a "back door" approach. No writer wants to write an overt commercial for your business. Even if they did, their editor wouldn't allow it. The best chance of success lies in promoting an article about something related but intriguing which will indirectly promote your business.

The press release should cover the most important points of your story first, and save the less important details for the end. This way, a busy journalist can quickly find the information he or she needs to decide whether to pursue your story. Answer the questions *What?, When?, Where?, How?,* and *Why?* Be sure to check your facts, and have another person review the release for clarity and punctuation.

You may also want to include a cover letter with your release. If at all possible, let the target of your correspondence know you're familiar with her work. Be explicit about the reason you're sending this release (i.e., "I saw your great article on coffee in *The Daily Planet,* and thought you might be interested in this story lead about…").

Follow up with the writers to whom you've sent your release. Call and ask if they have a moment to speak with you. If they respond by saying they're on deadline, pay attention. Ask when you can call back.

If the journalist does have time to chat, take advantage of the opportunity to build rapport. Then talk about the release and ask what questions they have. If the writer indicates she has no interest, express thanks and let her off the hook.

Most of the time and after a little practice, you'll find press people are grateful to have access to your expertise. They don't have the time to run around and keep their fingers on the pulse of *everything.* They need your help. You want theirs. P.R. is about relationships, and so is your business. Use one to help grow the other.

Sample Press Release

This sample release will give you an idea of what we mean by the What?, Where?, When?, How?, Why? approach. Use it as a model, or go to your local library and look for helpful book titles under Communications, Technical Writing, Public Relations, or Special Events Planning.

FOR IMMEDIATE RELEASE
October 10, 1995

ESPRESSO FUELS PRO PLAYOFF VICTORY
Players Seek Half-Time Boost at New Mocha Joe's

Seattle, WA — As their challenging first half came to a close, jerseys #7 and #10 made their way through the crowd at last night's critical playoff game and ordered two stiff drinks. One double short latte for the point guard, a grande five-shot Americano for the 6'10' power forward, and they powered back to the court to claim a 25-point victory.

Mocha Joe's Espresso complemented Seattle's Friday night win with their own grand opening score. The tall guys weren't the only ones in line; between the opening of the stadium doors and the final horn, a crowd of 587 coffee lovers visited the cart for espresso beverages. Espresso fans went through more than 33 pounds of espresso and over 76 gallons of milk.

"I've never seen anything like it," said Douglas Z. MacKinnon, a security guard at the Coliseum for 17 years. "Those fans were jazzed."

Conveniently located just inside and to the right of the main entrance, Mocha Joe's cart is the first of its kind at the Coliseum. The cart features a classic espresso menu, hot chocolate and steamed milk for kids, and sugar cookies shaped like basketballs from Seattle's Home Court Bakery. (No free throws, please.)

"We're looking forward to great success at the Coliseum," says Mocha Joe's owner and operator, Joe Monaghan. "We expect to open two more carts this season to make our exceptional products more accessible. We're very pleased to offer our services to such an enthusiastic public."

For more information about Mocha Joe's Espresso at the Coliseum and elsewhere, call (206) 555–8848, or write: Mocha Joe's, c/o Joe Monaghan, 238 South Broadway, Seattle, WA 98134.

####

Checklist: Marketing Your Operation

____ **Plan effective promotions**

    ____ Keep a list of clever marketing techniques you observe in and beyond your industry and region

    ____ Design your own creative marketing plan, reviewing pages 149–152 for ideas. Plan for:

        ____ Pre-opening

        ____ Grand opening

        ____ Ongoing promotions (seasonal specials, sponsorships, and other tactics that reinforce your identity)

    ____ Track customer response to these promotions

____ **Build positive public relations**

    ____ Collect articles by journalists/editors you think might be interested in a story about your business

    ____ When you believe you have a "story":

        ____ Prepare a press release

        ____ Write a letter that introduces you and the subject

        ____ Send these materials to a journalist(s)

        ____ Make follow-up calls to determine interest and proceed as appropriate

    ____ Try again

____ **Pay attention to aesthetics and appearance**

    ____ Keep your operation clean and attractive, focusing particular attention on:

        ____ Clarity of menu and pricing structure

        ____ Overall cleanliness

        ____ Avoiding clutter and keeping things organized

    ____ Schedule self-evaluations, and make adjustments as needed

    ____ Solicit customer feedback about appearance and service

CHAPTER 14
Maintaining
Your Equipment

Establishing a firm equipment maintenance program is a relatively simple and inexpensive way to contribute to the quality of your espresso operation. Although commercial espresso machines are built for rugged use, they are still machines. Regular maintenance will not only support espresso quality, but will reduce the frequency of necessary repair and help you avoid costly down-time.

There are two primary categories of maintenance: the kind you can do yourself, and the kind you can't.

Establishing a Cleaning Routine

The first maintenance category, the kind you can do yourself, is composed primarily of cleaning. Cleaning is not glamorous. It will, however, contribute significantly to the health of your operation.

In general, all the surfaces on the espresso machine should be kept spotless. Baristas should be wiping down the machine, cleaning and clearing the steam wands after each use, and rinsing their portafilters on an ongoing basis.

ESPRESSO MACHINE CLEANERS

Some cleaning activities—cleaning portafilter inserts and group screens, for example, and a part of your backflushing routine—

call for a special espresso machine cleaner. It is wise to invest in the kind of solution formulated specifically for these purposes.

Espresso machine cleaners foam when they come in contact with hot water. This foaming action scrubs and scours the hard-to-reach crannies on espresso machinery. The better espresso machine cleaners are biodegradable; ask for the Materials Data Safety Sheet (MSDS) on any cleaner for the low-down on its particulars. (See Appendix A for a list of espresso machine cleaner brands and sources.)

Avoid using liquid detergents, powdered dishwashing detergents, or Trisodiumphosphates (TSPs) on your espresso machine. These detergents are extremely hard to rinse away, and will leave a strong residue on your equipment.

BACKFLUSHING

The groups of the espresso machine should be backflushed regularly. Backflushing is the act of forcing water back up through the screens and group heads, and cleans places you can't reach any other way. Contrary to what some operators fear, there is absolutely no risk of polluting the boiler or coffee-brewing water during backflushing. The water cannot get that far.

To backflush, you need a blind filter—a filter insert without holes—or a rubber plug. (The plug, though adequate, doesn't work quite as well.) These accessories prevent the escape of water from the portafilter, thereby flushing water back into the machine. Backflushing can be done with or without using espresso cleaner, and over the course of a week should be done both ways. We recommend backflushing several times a day without cleaner, and once a week with it.

The steps are simple:

1. Replace the regular filter insert with a blind filter or plug.

2. Twist the portafilter firmly up into the group.

3. Activate the flow of water into the group, and run it steadily for 30–60 seconds. Then shut it off. It's a good idea to attend the group while doing this.

4. Activate the water flow again, this time pulsing it with several short bursts.

5. Grasp the handle of the portafilter firmly and reactivate the water flow. Use your grip on the handle to tighten and release, tighten and release, the portafilter in the group. This action forces out the coffee buildup around the group's sealing gasket.

The same result can be obtained by using the round head of a group cleaning brush to scrub the gasket during water flow. With either method, you will be splashing a great deal of very hot water around and may find it more comfortable to protect your fore-arms with a bar towel.

When backflushing with cleaner, place about one-half of a teaspoon of granular cleaner in the blind filter and execute steps 1–4 as described above. After rinsing any remaining cleaner out of the portafilter, do step 5 at least ten times to ensure that the group is completely rinsed.

Never attempt to backflush a manual or lever-operated espresso machine.

DRAIN TRAY, PORTAFILTERS, AND STEAM WANDS

To keep the drainage of brewing refuse unobstructed, pour a full pitcher of very hot water down the drain box at the end of the day. This refuse is usually composed of water and coffee sludge, and will clog the drainage tubes if allowed to cake or harden. If possible, pour the hot water over the length of the box and encourage it to drain by tilting the tray.

All removable brewing parts should be thoroughly cleaned each day as well. Take the filter inserts from each portafilter and the group screens from each group, soaking them in a pitcher of hot water for 10 to 15 minutes. Scrub these with a brush to rid the mesh and holes of all remaining grounds, then return them. Once a week, use a strong solution of espresso machine cleaner to soak both inserts and screens. Rinse well.

After a final wipe-down, steam wands should be left to soak in hot water overnight. Positioning a full mug or pitcher under each wand is the most convenient way to do this.

HOPPER AND DOSER

The dosing chamber of your espresso grinder should be brushed completely clean of residual coffee grounds at the end of each day. This prepares a clean, but dry, surface for tomorrow's fresh grounds.

The removable whole bean hopper at the top of the grinder should be washed with hot, soapy water. Rinse the hopper, then dry it thoroughly before replacing it on the grinder.

To maintain coffee freshness, it is important to keep all surfaces that come in contact with coffee before the actual brewing dry.

WATER TREATMENT DEVICES

You don't have to clean the filters or filter housings themselves, but it is in your best interest to keep your water clean by changing filters regularly. Construct a schedule for your operation, and follow it. Because most water treatment companies are eager to sell you filters, they'll help by reminding you how often, and when to start.

Water softening devices are a bit trickier because it's difficult to determine an exact schedule. Your individual calendar will vary with the hardness of your water and the specific device you use. Again, work with your supplier to come up with a firm plan. Then stick to it. You'll be doing your machine, your customers, and your business a big favor.

Scheduling Regular Maintenance Calls

The goal of scheduling service calls before you need them is to avoid down-time later on. There are several maintenance procedures that, if performed regularly, will enhance coffee quality and prevent the need for larger, more costly repair down the line. These procedures are best performed by an espresso machine supplier or service technician. As we emphasized earlier, make sure these suppliers keep a full inventory of parts on hand before you choose them as your providers. *Don't just take their word for it*—make them show you the workbench or parts board bursting with equipment. Ask them to convince you that they will be able to follow through on service commitments, both prescheduled and emergency.

There are two preventative maintenance routines we recommend adopting.

GASKET AND SCREEN REPLACEMENT, STEAM WAND REBUILD

Every six months, you should schedule a maintenance visit that will include:

- Replacement of portafilter gaskets
- Replacement of group screens (also called "diffuser screens")
- Steam wand valve rebuild/replacements
- Quick diagnostic checkup of electronic functions and programming

This visit usually takes about 1–2 hours, and costs around $150.00 (including labor). It's well worth it. These are the parts of your machine that take the most abuse—especially the steam wand valves. An ounce of prevention is worth, literally, a pound of cure. Performing these tasks regularly will keep your shots cleaner and tastier, and avoid damaging wear to the machine.

GRINDER BURR AND PORTAFILTER INSERT REPLACEMENT

Making these replacements proactively maintains espresso quality. These two procedures should be done at the same time, about every 1,000 to 1,200 pounds of coffee ground.

Grinder burrs need to be sharp to do their job. They wear over time, and if allowed to wear too far down they begin to crush coffee beans instead of grinding them. Crushed beans yield a decidedly inferior espresso.

The positioning, size, and shape of portafilter insert holes represent many years of engineering and experience, and are part of the ideal equation for brewing great espresso. Abrasion caused by the brewing process enlarges and reshapes these holes, which eventually sabotages the optimal balance of variables.

In Case of Emergency...

Make sure your employees know who to call. Put a sticker or magnet with service contacts on your espresso machine and near the water treatment system. List name, telephone number, and beeper number. Tell service technicians that you've done this, and that you trust they will answer employee requests promptly.

A Basic Troubleshooting Guide

Once you've got your espresso machine up and running, familiarize yourself and employees with this troubleshooting guide. Prepare a copy for your operations manual, or to keep in a drawer near the machine. This, too, will reduce operator panic, emergency service calls, and down-time.

SYMPTOM	PROBABLE CAUSE	REMEDIES
Coffee is brewing too slowly	• Pump pressure is incorrect (should be 8 to 9.5 bars)	✓ Adjust pump as necessary
	• Coffee grind is too fine	✓ Adjust grind (on grinder) to a coarser setting
	• Too much ground coffee used per dose	✓ Use doser on grinder
		✓ Reduce dosing amount on grinder
		✓ Stop "eyeballing" dose
	• Dispersion (group) screens are clogged	✓ Replace screens
	• Barista is tamping grounds too hard	✓ Lighten tamp
Coffee is brewing too fast	• Coffee grind is too coarse	✓ Adjust grind consistency (on grinder) to a finer setting
	• Too little coffee is being used per dose	✓ Use doser on grinder
		✓ Increase dosing amount on grinder
		✓ Stop "eyeballing" dose

SYMPTOM	PROBABLE CAUSE	REMEDIES
Coffee is brewing too fast (*continued*)	• Filter inserts are worn	✓ Replace filter
Water leaks around portafilter during brewing	• Collar where portafilter fits into machine has excessive coffee buildup	✓ Clean collar with stiff nylon brush
	• Portafilter gaskets are worn	✓ Call authorized technician to service inserts
Coffee grounds passing through portafilter into cup	• Grind is too fine	✓ Adjust grind (on grinder) to a coarser setting
	• Filter inserts worn	✓ Replace filter inserts
Drain tray overflows	• Drain box (under drain tray) is clogged	✓ Clean drain tray thoroughly
	• Drain hose is clogged	✓ Clear using air or water pressure, or very hot water
No steam pressure (gauge reads 0)	• Power to machine is interrupted	✓ Check circuit breaker
		✓ Check power cord plug
		✓ Check machine on/off switch
	• Heating element is not functioning	✓ Call authorized technician for service
	• Pressurestat is not functioning	✓ Call authorized technician for service

SYMPTOM	PROBABLE CAUSE	REMEDIES
Low steam pressure (gauge reads 1.0 to 1.5)	• Water level in steam boiler is too high	✓ Remove some water through hot water tap
		✓ Adjust autofill probe
	• Autofill system is not functioning	✓ Call authorized technician for service
	• Steam wands are clogged	✓ Clear holes in tip of steam wand with toothpick
		✓ Soak tip of steam wand in solution of espresso machine cleaner and hot water

Checklist: Daily Cleaning

_____ Backflush each group several times

_____ Pour a full pitcher of hot water down the drain box of the espresso machine

_____ Clean all removable brewing parts

_____ Brush grinder dosing chamber free of residual coffee grounds

Checklist: Weekly Cleaning

____ Backflush each group with espresso machine cleaner

____ Clean and soak inserts and screens in a strong solution of espresso machine cleaner

____ Wash removable whole bean hopper

Checklist: Ongoing Maintenance

_____ Change water filters regularly, according to the guidelines suggested by your local water treatment expert

_____ Inspect and change water softening devices according to the guidelines suggested by your local water treatment expert

_____ Schedule regular maintenance visits with your espresso machine technician for servicing of portafilter gaskets, group screens, steam wand valves, and machine electronics

_____ Replace grinder burr and portafilter inserts every 1,000 to 1,200 pounds

CHAPTER 15
Where Does the Time Go?

Either you can almost taste the foam on the top of your first cappuccino, or we lost you somewhere back in Chapter 4. If you are still with us, you're a graduate of sorts. You've just covered the groundwork necessary to start your own espresso business.

Use the following—and final—checklist to mark your progress. Some stages (in fact, many of them) must occur simultaneously, so the complete list should serve as an ongoing reminder about what needs to be kept in motion.

Edit the list to reflect any additional steps necessary for your individual operation. Tracking the entire process, and being scrupulous about fulfilling every step, will help you avoid unnecessary delays. And *that* will save you significant time and precious start-up capital.

Good job, and good luck. We wish you the greatest success as you move forward with your chosen venture.

Checklist: From Original Concept to Opening Day

_____ Choose your espresso business concept

_____ Develop business plan and identity (company name, logo, business cards)

_____ Establish criteria for location analysis (remembering health code considerations) and identify potential sites

_____ Prepare proposals for the landlords of at least five of these

_____ Negotiate lease with the landlord of choice

_____ Begin investigating equipment options, gathering specifications necessary to initiate permitting processes

_____ Engage in permitting and licensing process (with state, city, and federal governments, local health department)

_____ Calculate start-up costs

_____ Assess funding options and pursue the most favorable

_____ Shop for equipment: espresso machine and grinder(s), water treatment systems, espresso cart and drip brewer

_____ Determine menu

_____ Locate suppliers for coffee, dairy products, condiments and flavoring syrups, noncoffee beverage supplies, food, paper products and other renewables, utensils, signage, uniforms

_____ Design and begin implementing marketing plan

_____ Determine and fill personnel needs, preparing company, operational, and training materials as necessary

_____ Prepare for grand opening

_____ Stock, set up, and get ready to go....

_____ OPEN!

A P P E N D I X   A

Espresso Industry Resources

As is the case in any rapidly expanding industry, the list of quality suppliers in the espresso sector shifts and expands regularly. At the time of printing, these are the ones we recommend. Use additional industry resources, such as magazines and trade shows, to keep abreast of new products and players.

Although some products are sold directly from the factory, many brands are distributed by regional sales people or independent whole salers. Don't be surprised if your first call is answered with the name of a regional distributor—or the second, a more local source. Exact distribution methods change as individual markets shift and grow. The information that follows, in most cases listing contact specifics for importers or corporate headquarters, will get you started.

ESPRESSO MACHINE BRANDS

La Marzocco, Rio, Astoria
Espresso Specialists, Inc.
4544 Leary Way N W
Seattle, WA 98107
(206) 784-9563
fax (206) 784-9582

Faema
Faema Corporation of America
P.O. Box 522
Stamford, CT 06904
(203) 323-5040
(800) 443-2362
fax (203) 323-6183

Rancilio, La San Marco, La Cimbali
These brands do not maintain centralized U.S. offices. Check with the espresso and coffee equipment suppliers in your area to locate distributors.

Brasilia
Rosito and Bisani Imports, Inc.
940 S. LaBrea
Los Angeles, CA 90036
(213) 937-1888
(800) 848-4444
fax (213) 938-0728

La Pavoni
Crossroads Espresso
882 Mahler Rd.
Burlingame, CA 94010
(415) 342-1111
(800) 552-4424
fax (415) 697-6464

Reneke
Boyd's Coffee Company/Techni-Brew
19730 N.E. Sandy Blvd.
Portland, OR 97230
(503) 666-4545
(800) 545-4077
fax (503) 669-2223

Unic
Illycaffe Espresso
15455 Greenway-Hayden Loop #7
Scottsdale, AZ 85260
(602) 951-0466
fax (602) 483-8631

DOSER-GRINDER BRANDS

Astoria, Rio
Espresso Specialists, Inc.
4544 Leary Way N.W.
Seattle, WA 98107
(206) 784-9563

Mazzer
Illycaffe Espresso
15455 Greenway-Hayden Loop #7
Scottsdale, AZ 85260
(602) 951-0466
fax (602) 483-8631

Rossi
Rosito and Bisani Imports, Inc.
940 S. LaBrea
Los Angeles, CA 90036
(213) 937-1888
(800) 848-4444
fax (213) 938-0728

Faema
Faema Corporation of America
P.O. Box 522
Stamford, CT 06904
(203) 323-5040
(800) 443-2362
fax (203) 323-6183

WATER TREATMENT EXPERTS

Everpure
660 Blackhawk Dr.
Westmont, IL 60559

(708) 654-4000
fax (708) 654-1115

Filtercold Inc.
1840 E. University Dr.
Tempe, AZ 85281
(602) 894-2941
fax (602) 894-5485

Culligan
1 Culligan Parkway
Northbrook, IL 60062
(708) 205-6000
fax (708) 205-6030

Cuno Inc.
400 Research Parkway
Meridan, CT 06450
(203) 237-5541
fax (203) 238-8716

The Water System Group
4051 Glencoe Ave., Unit 3
Marina del Rey, CA 90292
(800) 350-9283
fax (31) 305-0374

Bunn O Matic*
1400 Stephenson Dr.
Springfield, IL 62708
(800) 637-8606
(217) 529-6622

*Bunn O Matic has a filter system designed especially for coffee
equipment; their products work well for espresso machines also.

ESPRESSO CART MANUFACTURERS

Pedrola Manufacturing
12108 Highway 525, Suite B-4
Mukilteo, WA 98275
(206) 743-4671
(800) 795-CART
fax (206) 745-1843

Storecrafters, Inc.
6103-A NE St. James
Vancouver, WA 98663
(206) 737-0433
(800) 593-2723
fax (206) 737-9661

Design Line Manufacturing
14220 N.E. 193rd Pl. #B
Woodinville, WA 98072
(206) 489-2559
fax (206) 485-6380

Bernhard Woodwork Ltd.
3670 Woodhead Dr.
Northbrook, IL 60062
(708) 291-1040
fax (708) 291-1184

Carts of Colorado
5750 Holly St.
Denver, CO 80216
(303) 288-1000
fax (303) 286-8539

ESPRESSO ACCESSORY SUPPLIERS (MAIL ORDER)

Espresso Supply
P.O. Box 70602
Seattle, WA 98107
(206) 782-6670
(800) 782-6671
fax (206) 789-8221

Coffee Relatives, Inc.
380 Swift Ave. #19
South San Francisco, CA 94080
(415) 952-6200

Espresso Carts Parts N.W.
618 7th Ave. S.E.
Olympia, WA 98501
(800) 459-5594

Visions Espresso Service
1500 1st Ave. S.
Seattle, WA 98134
(206) 623-6709
fax (206) 623-6710

ESPRESSO MACHINE CLEANERS

PuroCaff
Pacific Espresso
623 Soquel Ave.
Santa Cruz, CA 95062
(800) 782-6671
fax (408) 459-0798

Visions Espresso Cleaner
Visions Espresso Service
1500 1st Ave. S.
Seattle, WA 98134
(206) 623-6709
fax (206) 623-6710

E.S.P.
National Chemicals
105 Liberty Ave.
Winona, MN 55987
(507) 454-5640
(800) 533-0027
fax (507) 454-5641

COFFEE ROASTERS BY REGION

NORTHWEST

Batdorf & Bronson
510 Columbia St.
Olympia, WA 98501
(800) 955-5282
fax (206) 754-5243

Caffe D'Arte
719 S. Myrtle St.
Seattle, WA 98108
(206) 762-4381
fax (206) 763-4665

Caravalli Coffees
18405 72nd Ave. S.
Kent, WA 98032
(206) 251-9256
fax (206) 251-9257

Espresso Vivace
901 E. Denny Way
Seattle, WA 98122
(206) 860-5869
fax (206) 860-1567

K & F Fine Coffees
600 N.E. Couch St.
Portland, OR 97232
(503) 234-7788
fax (503) 231-9827

Kobos Coffee
5620 S.W. Kelly Ave.
Portland, OR 97201
(503) 246-8883
fax (503) 246-0940

Seattle's Best Coffee
1333 Stewart St.
Seattle, WA 98109
(206) 624-8858
fax (206) 682-3143

Starbucks Coffee Company
2203 Airport Way S.
Seattle, WA 98134
(206) 447-1575
(800) 447-1575

Southwest

Allegro Coffee Company
1930 Central Ave.
Boulder, CO 80301
(800) 666-4869
fax (303) 449-5259

Caribbean Coffee
116 E. Yanonali St.
Santa Barbara, CA 93101
(805) 962-3201
fax (805) 962-5074

Daybreak Coffee
4406-C 19th St.
Lubbock, TX 79407
(806) 799-1994
fax (806) 799-1995

Diedrich Coffee
350 Clinton St. Ste. A
Costa Mesa, CA 92626
(714) 438-2294
fax (714) 434-6276

Illycaffe Espresso
15455 Greenway-Hayden Loop #7
Scottsdale, AZ 85260
(602) 951-0466
fax (602) 483-8631

Spinnelli Coffee Co.
495 Barneveld Ave.
San Francisco, CA 94124
(415) 821-7100
fax (415) 821-7199

Thanksgiving Coffee
P.O. Box 1918
Fort Bragg, CA 95437
(800) 462-1999
fax (707) 964-0351

MIDWEST

The Coffee Barrel
2446 Jolly Rd.
Okemos, MI 48864
(517) 349-3888
fax (517) 349-3036

Mid-America Coffee Specialties
13044 Skypark Dr.
Omaha, NE 68137
(800) 597-7376
fax (402) 895-7669

Steep and Brew
855 E. Broadway
Madison, WI 53716
(608) 223-0707
fax (608) 256-1244

NORTHEAST

Dallis Bros., Inc.
100-30 Atlantic Ave.
Ozone Park, NY 11416
(718) 845-3010
fax (718) 843-0178

Excellent Coffee
259 East Ave.
Pawtucket, RI 02860
(800) 345-2007
fax (401) 724-0560

Green Mountain Coffee
33 Coffee Lane
Waterbury, VT 05676
(802) 244-5621
fax (802) 244-5436

MIDDLE EAST COAST

Mill Mountain Coffee
700 N. Main St.
Blacksburg, VA 24060
(703) 552-7442

Monaco Espresso
4710 Bethesda Ave.
Bethesda, MD 20814
(301) 913-0113
fax (301) 907-0015

Quartermain Coffee Roasters
4972 Wyaconda Rd.
Rockville, MD 20852
(301) 961-1570
fax (301) 961-1563

SOUTHEAST

Aurora Coffee
313 N. Highland Ave.
Atlanta, GA 30307
(404) 351-6711
fax (404) 351-6711

Broad Street Coffee Roasters
P.O. Box 333
Chapel Hill, NC 27514
(919) 933-9933
fax (919) 933-9933

Joffrey's Coffee
4517 West Ohio
Tampa, FL. 33614
(813) 875-5198
fax (813) 873-1403

COFFEE COMPANIES THAT SUPPLY POD ESPRESSO

Green Mountain Coffee Company (see above, Northeast)

Illycaffe Espresso (see above, Southwest)

Excellent Coffee Company (see above, Northeast)

ESPRESSO TRAINING AND OPERATIONS RESOURCES

Java U (manual series)
1306 Western Ave. Suite 406
Seattle, WA 98101
(800) 405-2828
fax (206) 623-0446

Making a Mountain of Money Out of a Hill of Beans (book)
by Jill Edwards
Caffe Andiamo
545 Rainier Blvd. Ste. 14
Seattle, WA 98027
(206) 557-8331

Kaladi Coffee Academy (training video and workbook)
6921 Brayton Dr., Ste. A
Anchorage, AK 99507
(800) 770-5483
fax (907) 344-5935

Espresso 101, Spilling the Beans (video tapes)
Bellissimo Media Productions
1800 Valley River Dr., Ste. 101
Eugene, OR 97401
(503) 683-5373
(800) 655-3955
fax (503) 683-1010

ESPRESSO FRANCHISE OPPORTUNITIES

Barista Brava
1150 17th St. N.W., 5th Floor
Washington, DC 20036
(202) 331-0962
fax (202) 331-0964

Joffrey's Coffee & Tea Co.
4517 W. Ohio Ave.
Tampa, FL 33614-7768
(813) 875-5198
(800) 458-JAVA
fax (813) 873-1403

Caffè Appassionato
4001 21st Ave. W.
Seattle, WA 98199
(206) 281-8040
fax (206) 282- 9544

INDUSTRY PUBLICATIONS AND PROFESSIONAL ORGANIZATIONS

Specialty Coffee Association
One World Trade Center,
Ste. 800
Long Beach, CA 90831-0800
(310) 983-8090

Café Olé Magazine
150 Nickerson, Ste. 201
Seattle, WA 98109
(206) 217-9773

CoffeeTalk
1306 Western, Ste. 406
Seattle, WA 98101
(206) 382-2112
fax (206) 623-0446
email: ctmag@halcyon.com

Fresh Cup
P.O. Box 82817
Portland, OR 97282-0817
(503) 224-8544

Tea & Coffee Trade Journal
130 W. 42nd St., 22nd Floor
New York, NY 10036
(212) 391-2060

Uker's Guide to Coffee & Tea
130 W. 42nd St., 22nd Floor
New York, NY 10036
(212) 391-2060

World Coffee & Tea
1801 Rockville Pike, Ste. 330
Rockville, MD 20852
(301) 984-7333

A P P E N D I X   B

A Basic Espresso Glossary

Adjusting collar—a component of the grinder that is rotated by the operator to increase or decrease the fineness or coarseness of the ground coffee.

Autofill—a feature of many espresso machines that automatically controls and maintains the water level inside the boiler.

Barista—Italian for bartender; In the U.S., a person who operates an espresso machine and prepares espresso beverages.

Bean hopper—the cone-shaped chamber on the top of an espresso grinder that holds whole bean coffee.

Boiler pressure gauge—the instrument used to determine the steam pressure within an espresso machine boiler.

Breve—a term used to describe a drink made with steamed half and half (for example: breve latte, breve cappuccino)

Brew button pad—control switches on an automatic espresso machine that correspond to the desired shot size and quanity (i.e., single ristretto, single shot, double shot).

Burr—see "grinder burr."

Caffe latte—one or more servings of espresso, with steamed milk to the top of the cup and a 1/4" finish of steamed milk foam.

Caffe macchiato—"marked" in Italian; one or more "ristretto" shots poured over the same combination of steamed milk and foam used to make a caffe latte.

Caffe mocha—one or more servings of espresso mixed with the appropriate amount of chocolate syrup, then filled with steamed milk and topped with a flourish of whipped cream.

Cappuccino—one or more servings of espresso in a cup, topped with equal parts steamed and frothed milk.

Condiments—anything added to complement the primary fare. Where espresso beverages are concerned, condiments usually include but are not limited to half and half, sugar, and a range of powdered spices and/or flavorings sprinkled on top of drinks. The most popular of these are cocoa, cinnamon, nutmeg, and vanilla.

Demitasse—a small porcelain or china cup traditionally used to serve straight espresso; usually 1.5–3 ounces in size.

Demitasse spoon—a small spoon provided alongside demitasse cup and saucer; used for stirring sweetener into espresso.

Diffusion block—a component that diffuses hot brewing water as it passes from the group casting.

Dispersion screen—a mesh screen that provides the final diffusion of hot brewing water after it passes through the diffusion block and before it reaches the ground coffee.

Dome lid—a specially shaped plastic lid used on thermal takeout cups; accommodates the extra loft of an espresso drink.

Doser—the device mounted on a grinder that measures and dispenses ground coffee into the portafilter for brewing.

"Double" or *double-shot*—refers to a beverage that contains two shots of espresso (for example, a "double latte").

Dry—describes an espresso beverage made with a greater-than-usual proportion of foam, most often used in conjunction with a cappuccino.

Espresso—very strong coffee brewed one ounce at a time, rapidly extracted from finely ground coffee at very high temperature and pressure on an espresso machine. The word "espresso" can also refer to a special blend of coffees formulated for use on the espresso machine ("espresso blend"), or the distinctly dark roast typically applied to an espresso blend ("espresso roast").

Espresso machine—the machine used to prepare espresso coffee beverages.

Extraction—the process of passing hot water through ground coffee; this process transforms soluble coffee elements to beverage form.

Extraction time—the amount of time that hot water remains in contact with ground coffee during extraction.

Filter insert—the stainless steel filter basket that forms the inside cup of the portafilter; used to contain coffee grounds during the brewing process. Typically found in single, double, and triple shot configurations.

Flavoring syrup—a very sweet syrup used to flavor coffee beverages after the brewing process.

Foam—steamed milk that has been aerated to create light froth.

Grande—typically, the largest drink size available; 16 ounces.

Granita—a flavored, slush-type drink often served by espresso operators, and requiring special equipment to prepare.

Grinder—the machine used to grind or mill coffee beans into granular or powdered form.

Grinder burrs—the sharp steel plates within the grinder that cut or mill coffee beans.

Group—a brewing head, or port, on the espresso machine.

Insert—see "filter insert."

Group casting—a component of the espresso machine group in which the portafilter is inserted for brewing. Usually made of cast brass, for even heat conduction.

Group portafilter gasket—the gasket that provides a seal when the portafilter is inserted into the group casting.

Insert retaining spring—a small wire spring clip that holds the filter insert in the portafilter.

Knockbox—the container into which spent coffee grounds are "knocked," or dispensed.

Latte—the Italian word for milk; slang for caffe latte (for example, "I'd like a latte, please!").

Manual fill valve—the device used to manually introduce water into the boiler of an espresso machine.

Milk thermometer—a thermometer of specific range used to monitor the temperature of steaming milk.

Over-extraction—a term that describes excess water or extraction time used during the brewing process; yields an overly acidic and bitter espresso.

Pod—a pre-ground, individually packaged serving of espresso; usually requires special equipment for brewing.

Portafilter—the coffee handle, or filter handle, of the espresso machine; contains filter insert and is twisted up into a group for brewing.

Pump pressure gauge—the instrument used to determine the pump, or extraction, pressure of brewing water on an espresso machine.

Ristretto—a short or "restricted" shot of espresso, typically 3/4 of an ounce.

"Single," or single shot—describes an espresso beverage containing one shot of espresso (for example, a "single tall latte," or a "single espresso").

Shot—a single serving of brewed espresso, usually 1–1.5 ounces.

Skinny—slang for a beverage made with skim or nonfat milk

Steam valve—the device on an espresso machine used to control the flow of steam into milk during the steaming process.

Steam wand—a pipe-like extension of stainless steel with a nozzle-type tip from which steam exits the espresso machine and is introduced to milk.

Tall—refers to a medium-sized beverage, typically 12 ounces.

Tamp—the process of pressing ground coffee into the filter insert just prior to brewing.

Tamper—the device used for tamping.

Under-extraction—a term that describes insufficient water or extraction time during the brewing process; under-extraction yields a watery espresso with grossly underdeveloped flavors.

Wet—describes an espresso beverage made with a less-than-usual proportion of foam, most often used to describe a customized cappuccino.

INDEX